Extinguisher

Letters of Extinguisher

Extinguisher

Letters of Extinguisher

ISBN/EAN: 9783337031084

Printed in Europe, USA, Canada, Australia, Japan

Cover: Foto ©ninafisch / pixelio.de

More available books at **www.hansebooks.com**

LETTERS

OF

"EXTINGUISHER."

———⋘◇⋙———

SINGAPORE:

PRINTED FOR THE AUTHOR

AT THE "MISSION PRESS" OFFICE.

1 8 7 0.

G. DANKER PRINTER, MISSION PRESS—SINGAPORE.

DEDICATED

To the Subjects of these Epistles,

TRUSTING THAT THEY WILL RECEIVE

THEM IN THE SPIRIT WITH WHICH THEY

WERE WRITTEN.

EXTINGUISHER.

PREFACE.

EXTINGUISHER UNTO HIS FRIENDS GREETING;

Inasmuch as some among you have asked of me
to publish these my Epistles, place I them before
you, believing that you asked it not from their worth
as writings, but as an echo of your own minds.

"WHAT IS WRIT IS WRIT;
WOULD IT WERE WORTHIER."

LETTERS

OF

EXTINGUISHER.

SIR,—In the Island of Singapore, that lieth over against Malacca, which is in the far Indies, in the days of the reign of Col. Cavena', there dwelt many great and good men who were called Government Officials, because that they fished all they could out of the Government.

But among these was one possessed of a little soul, who thought himself larger than other men, and wished others to think even as he did.

And he said unto himself: What shall I do that I may cause my name to be heard, and make myself to be great, even above my brother officials?

And he went about seeking how he might encompass his designs.

And it so happened that this man whose name was Mustirattindint, of the tribe of the Scots, had among his other duties with the vessels which traded in merchandize with far countries, (and which lay in the harbour near Singapore), to see that the lamps of these vessels were trimmed and lighted when darkness covered the face of the Earth.

Now this was done on the land by Celestials which resemble men, save that they have tails, but on the water was it this man's work.

And as he wandered along the shores of the Sea he espied many of these carriers of merchandize with no light.

And he said unto himself: I have not told unto those men who command these vessels that they must show a *Burning* light, so tomorrow they will do even as to-day, and I will come down upon them in the dead of night with a lead pencil, and I will take the names of these vessels, and of their wicked masters, (who, peradventure, are like unto the foolish virgins) and I will bind them that they pay unto me fifty shekels of silver, even fifty pieces of silver from each vessel, so that my name may shine like a *burning* light throughout the land.

Now it all came to pass even as he had said unto himself, and the men of the sea did pay each man fifty shekels of silver, but a cry went up from among these men, because of this unjust deed.

Now it came to pass that this wail reached even to the ears of the Governor, who was a just man in all his walks, and who was called Cavena' (after the manner of the Scots) because that he would *never* "*cave in*" to the wrong.

And he sent for Mustirattindint and said unto him. Why hast thou done this wrong thing?

And Mustirattindint answered and said " Lo, I thought to do that which was pleasant and good in thy sight, and now thou upbraidest me. And the Governor answered him saying, Give back unto these men of the sea every shekel that thou hast taken so unjustly from them.

Then Mustirattindint subsided: And he went out from the presence of the Governor.

1st Feby. 1866.

IN *re* DAVIDSON *vs:* ORD. ✕

"THE LAWYERS' FIX" OR "HOW I WOULD HAVE DONE IT."

By Extinguisher

In One Act—One Scene.

PERSONS REPRESENTED.

Col. Mc F.—Judge of Supreme Court.
Falstaff ⎫
Kayu Puti ⎬ Lawyers.
Kayu Puti Kitchil ⎭
Sheriff

SCENE—COURT ROOM, SINGAPORE.

Enter Lawyers and Sheriff.

Sheriff.—" Good morning all ! I come with noose prepared to snare the Lawyers."

Falstaff.—" Take care, good Sir, that thou in thy warm zeal, entangle not thyself, for lawyers are not birds to be by such chaff caught."

Enter Col. Mc F. with big books bound in calf under his arm.

Col. Mc F.—" How now, ye fiends ! dare ye in sacred Court of
Justice wrangle thus ? know ye that in my power it lies, for this
contempt of Court to send ye all to " quod"! One of your number
lies there now for conduct similar, pale and wan with rings of iron
on his legs, counting the weary hours as they do drag their tedious
length along, with nought but B. and S. to keep his spirits up ; to
keep these up, he puts the spirits down. Silence then, all, and hear
me well, while I do mete out justice.

(Gets poetical) " To me for Writ of Habeas Corpus, one Falstaff
" has applied, to let the Son of David from vile durance slide. In
" Law I am not deep, and so, for two whole nights, I've had no
" wink of sleep, but through these stupid books have sought to find,
" some precedent of case like this defined." (Turning to Sheriff)
" Sheriff ! hast thou the Corpus safe in hand, which these litigious
" men of me demand "?

Sheriff.—" My Lud ! I have it not ; though I do hear it lingers
" still in quod, and clanks its chains, while vowing vengeance."

Judge.—" You have it not ? Oh ! then the case looks queer"?
(Turns over pages of Blackstone) " but jovial Blackstone makes
" the point quite clear." " So"! tome 2 page 9, case Doe and Roe"
(reads) " When one has not a corpus in his charge, he cannot give
" it up to go at large." " This wise assertion seems to me quite
" grand, and shows me just exactly how I stand. I therefore
" cannot give the writ y'apply for, if for non-issue, I it die for."

Kayu Puti, Kayu Puti Kitchil, Falstaff, *loq:*—
" Fudge ! who in the de'il ever saw such Judge."

Judge.—" What dared ye say ! ! For this contempt of Court,
" I will to quod the whole of ye transport ; and now are left no
" more bold men of sin (whom all agree to heaven they do'nt let
" in) so 't strikes me I've now spoiled your little sport, and hold
" ye where the wool is very short, for none remain to ask for you
" a writ ; now, Sheriff, see they *all to Jail do flit.*"

(Exeunt Lawyers in charge of dark Policemen).

Judge *(getting prosy)* Now *Justice* reigns supreme, and *Law*
shall not again these portals darken !

(Exit with salute of 21 guns)

Exeunt Omnes.

ACT I. SCENE I.

Town Hall—Benicia.

Enter

GOVERNOR SAHARA.

(So called on account of place of birth.)

CHIEF JUSTICE.

HEADS OF DEPARTMENTS.

HON'BLE MEN.

Gov. loq.—In this our forum have we met, that we in confab close may quietly discuss the "freedom of the press." As for myself I do object to't.

Heads of Departments.—It doth us proud that we, with your Celestial Highness, should agree. We all, in thy majestic person, are made one, and therefore 'tis for us to speak but as thine echo.

Tummus Skot.—(for the Honorable men.) Well—Rubbut is an honorable man, yea, both of us are honorable men, and therefore will we not, in clamor, raise our voices? In fine, why *should* we leave our gods, the dollars and the cents, to mix in such Celestial company?

Our voices are but as the wind, and when the Governor does ope his mouth, the deed is done.

Why, therefore, should we waste our valuable time in useless protests?

Capt. of Vol. Host. loq.—I'll tell thee why, mine honorable brother.

Is't not a goodly sight to see our names on all our chits with glorious "honorable" superscribed? And those among us, who did leave their country for their country's good, can thus be lost to sight, for 'mongst our kinsfolk dear 'twould *never* sure be dreamed that we were honorable. We then among them may appear in high estate, and with this foreign name attached to ours, we may in time, *in our own fatherland*, be thus considered.

Chief Justice.—I must remind my honorable brothers, that they from off the matter have departed, yet as my Scottish friend awhile ago did say, it matters little what he thinks or speaks upon the subject. Why not then end the farce, and let the great Mogul at once say " Thus it is," and there the matter's settled ?

As for myself, I think it best that we among us have no Members of the press our crude words to report.	From what I've seen thus far, but few there are among us who can frame a speech, while far the greater part like Logs do sit, until the Governor speaks his mind, and then the Logs with one accord, through magnetism wonderful, jump to the same conclusion with His Majesty.

I therefore think, that Members of the Press should be excluded, from all of our debates, until the moment that His Excellency shall speak, and then they have the matter settled without further waste of valuable time.

Governor,—I move that Members of the Press with note-books in their hands be not admitted.

Attorney General.—Most righteous judgment!

Auditor General.—Wisdom personified!

Treasurer General.—The very words I should have used!

Colonial Secy. & Engineer,—Of course!

Clerk of Councils,—I had already entered it as law, so soon as I did hear his Highness speak.

Adjourned for cool drinks,

Singapore, 18th June, 1868.

CHRONICLES OF ST. GEORGE.

CHRONICLES OF ST. GEORGE.

CHAPTER I.

I. IN the days of Victoria, Queen of England, there dwelt certain of her subjects in the Island of a distant sea, and it being so far removed from her throne, she sent unto them a Governor that he might rule over them in her name.

2 Now this Governor had but one leg, for said Victoria unto herself: It is but a small place, therefore will I not send a whole man unto them.

3. And when the Governor was come unto this Island which is called Singapura, after the manner of the Malays even unto this day, he did rule the people of Victoria with a just hand.

4. And he shewed kindness unto them, even like unto the kindness of a woman.

5. Then the people of Victoria did murmur among themselves, and said one unto another—What manner of man is this that has been sent to rule over us? His ways are too easy that he should be permitted to rule over men: Rather let him be in charge of a land of women and children, but send unto us a man in whom dwelleth some "snap."

6. And they did write unto their Queen even as they spoke.

7. Now when Victoria heard these things she did even as they asked, and she sent unto these people a new Governor.

8. And the new Governor did as he was commanded, and went unto them to preside over them.

9. And when he was arrived, he called a carpenter unto him and commanded him that he should make unto him a throne.

10. Now throne in the language of the Dictionary is a chair of State, but in the language of the world it signifies a seat of Royalty.

11. So the people were wroth, and said among themselves, What is it that this man doeth? Shall he make himself a King over us?

12. And they with one accord declared that he should be sent from among them, even into the land of Coventry should he be sent-

13. But the Governor mounted his throne, and the people agreed to wait yet a little longer.

14. Now the Governor being a wise man, said unto himself, This place is surrounded with water, and how can I remove myself and my goods when it seems good unto me.

15. And he looked about him, and behold the only vessel he could find, which was of the chattels of the former Governor had no bottom, and the screw was loose.

16. And he called the Elders of the people unto him, and spake saying: What shall I do that I may have a steamer worthy of my royalty.

17. And they with one accord replied: Lay taxes upon the people, and buy such an one as seems good unto our master.

18. And he went out and bought, and paid 60,000 shekels of silver.

19. But the end was not yet.

20. And it came to pass, that as he wandered through the chambers of his palace, his leg went through the floor, even into the chamber below protruded his leg.

21. And one of his servants standing near, seeing what had happened, cried out, Master! would that I might suffer in thy stead.

22. And the Governor was sore vexed and summoned the Elders of the people again before him, and said unto them, What is this thing that you have done unto me? Behold the house that you have prepared for me is rotten, even unto the beams. Is it that you desire to have another one legged Ruler over you?

23. And the Elders of the people trembled before him, and answered: Master lay more taxes upon thy servants, and buy land and pull down houses and build such a temple as seemeth good unto thee.

24. And he did even as they said unto him.

25. And the land was filled with sorrow, for the pockets of the people were tender, and they lifted up their voices, and cried with one accord, " Let him go from among us, lest we all starve."

CHAPTER II.

1. Now this Governor had been a ruler over Convicts, and the ways and customs of good and free men were new unto him.

2. And he passed many laws, that were obnoxious unto the people.

3. Now the Governor was a man of letters, and could read.

4. And he read a parchment which told of the feudal times.

5. Now he did see that in those days travellers were ofttime detained by feudal lords and cast into dungeons, and it remembered the Governor of his own former time, and he was pleased.

6. Then said he unto himself. "Have I not had my own will thus far in all things—wherefore then should I not be like unto those men of old?"

7. Lo! I will make a law, and it shall give me power even greater than the power of the Queen.

8. And it shall be in this wise; when any man, who is not of the people of Victoria sheweth himself in my dominions, and I like him not; then shall it be that I will send unto him a chit and will order him that he travel.

9. And if he travel not, then I will cast him into a dungeon, and there shall be none to release him.

10. For I will put an end to the old law, even an end to the *Habeas Corpus*.

11. Now there were much people in the land of Singapura which were not of the house of Victoria.

12. And they marvelled greatly, and began to say among themselves "Is it not better for us that we skedaddle. Verily this man is possessed of an evil spirit."

CHAPTER III.

In answer to "Snuffers" and "John Brown" who called in question the right of "Extinguisher," being a foreigner, to criticise the acts of Government.

1. Now at that time there arose certain scribes who called themselves Snuffers, and they did make light of the writings of a Philosopher of the period.

2. And the Philosopher was called the Extinguisher,—because that he labored to extinguish whatever seemed wrong in the customs of his friends.

3. Moreover, he was a good man and his walks were in the paths of virtue.

4. Now when the Governor of the Island of Singapura did do

those things which seemed wrong in the eyes of Extinguisher, he did speak his mind on all these acts.

5. And it was not done in a spirit of bitterness, neither was it to bring derision upon the rulers, but that the rulers might see how those subject to them, did look upon their acts, and that they might be brought to think more deeply upon them.

6. Now this Philosopher was perhaps in the wrong, but he had a head even like unto the head of a Governor, and is it not written that two heads are better than one, even if one is a sheep's head?

7. So he did write.

8. And when the Snuffers did see what was written, they murmured at it because the Philosopher was not of the House of Victoria, and was a stranger among them.

9. But the Progenitors of the Philosopher were of the same blood, and he felt like a brother among them.

10. Moreover he spake the same tongue.

11. And it came to pass that when it was seen what was spoken by the Snuffers, there arose great indignation among certain of the people.

12. And the days of the Snuffers were numbered—And the days of the last of the Snuffers, after that he was discovered, were two, and he died.

13. And there was no one to mourn for them.

14. Then arose John Brown, No. 93, and he did also write and speak against this good man.

15. And he was a man of ignorance and could not spell.

16. Moreover his Uncle, called George, was a man of sin, and was stoned to death because that he did cheat a young virgin of her small change.

17. And the days of John Brown after that he had written were three, and he died.

18. And there was great rejoicing because that there was now none left to abuse

EXTINGUISHER.

CHAPTER IV.

1 And it came to pass that a ship which was in the waters that encompassed Singapura did take fire.

2. Now this ship had cost much money and the body of it was filled with cotton, which merchandize was of great price so that

there was much consternation in the island when the news was noised abroad.

3. When Mustirattindint heard this thing he hurried to the seaside, for it was one of the duties of this man to put out fires in the harbor.

4. And he reasoned within himself, and said : Lo ! now is a good time to make our Ruler appear well in the eyes of the people. Did he not tell unto them of how much use the new vessel would be unto them, even the ' Peiho,' (for that was her name.) And straightway he went on board the ' Peiho,' and did take the burning vessel in tow, and did pilot her unto a safe anchorage.

5. And the people said : Surely this vessel *is* of some use.

6. But when the Governor heard it, he was wroth, and he sent unto Mustirattindint that he should come before him.

7. And when he was come, he rebuked him, saying : What manner of thing is this : Is my yacht to be as a pilot boat, even as a tug to the vessels of my subjects.

8. And Mustirattindint answered him never a word, but felt mixed.

9. And the end was not yet.

10. Now it was that in the days of the former Ruler, the Christian Brethren had agreed among themselves that they would build a house.

11. And the Christian Brethren were good and pure men, who had done much good in the Colony, so that all men looked upon them kindly, howbeit their worship was not as the worship of the children of Victoria.

12. And the chief Ruler had promised unto them bricks to build their house.

13. And it was agreed that a certain class of Government Officials, called Convicts, should make these bricks, and that the Brethren should pay for them only so much as they did cost.

14. Now when the new Ruler was come they went unto him and said, Master, we be come for our bricks, even the bricks that were agreed upon by Colonel Cavenagh.

15. And they showed him the promise of the Colonel in writing.

16. But he answering said unto them : I do not know him of whom you speak, for he departed from the coast ere I came, and I did not have the pleasure of an introduction, neither is his handwriting known unto me.

17. Behold now shall ye make your bricks without straw even as was commanded of the Israelites of old.

18. And they departed from his presence.

19. And the children of Victoria were sad, for the Christian Brethren were poor, and bricks were cheap, and they felt that the word of the former Ruler in such matter should have been sacred.

CHAPTER V.

1. And it came to pass that a disturbance arose in the land of the Betelnuts which being interpreted is Penang.

2. And the Chief Ruler hearing thereof and finding the climate of Singapura rather warm, betook himself to that country.

3. Now when he arrove there, the troubles had continued nigh unto fourteen days, and there had been murder and rapine abroad, and no man knew the number that had been slain.

4. But none of the men of the land of Jonbool were hurt, for the troubles were among two tribes of the Celestials, called the Goins and the Topi Kongs.

5. But much of the property of the men of Jonbool was destroyed, and they cast about to find how they should make good their losses.

Now the Governor was a man of snap, and possessed of a spirit called Bak Bone.

6. And he called unto him the chief men of the Goins and the Topi Kongs, and said unto them : Why have ye allowed this wrong thing.

7. And they answering said . How could it have been prevented by us.

8. And he answered : Lo! are ye not the rulers over these tribes, and can these things be, if ye set your faces against them ?

9. And they spake in their defence, saying : Lo! have you not a tribe called Fanyuns in the country called Ouldairen in the land of Jonbool.

10. And is not Victoria the head man of the Fanyuns, as also of all the tribes of Jonbool. Why, then, shall you not make her responsible for the Fanyuns, even as you would make us answer for the deeds of the Goins and the Topi Kongs.

11. And he answering said : Ye have spoken well, and right dwelleth on your side. Nevertheless, I would show my power unto the men of all lands.

12. And ye shall each of you pay unto me 10,000 shekels of silver, and shall make good the property which has been destroyed by the Goins and the Topi Kongs.

13. And ye shall be cast into utter darkness, until the money be paid.

14. And he cast them into prison.

15. Now when the news came unto the coast of Singapura of what things the Governor had done, the people wondered much.

16. For it was written in the laws of the land of Jonbool that no ruler of the land should take upon himself to do such deeds.

17. And it came to the ears of a notable pleader called John, whose surname was Hatchsoon, because of his appearance.

18. [For is it not written that coming events cast their shadows before.]

19. Therefore was he called Hatchsoon.

20. And John said within himself: This Governor has done those things which are not lawful: And he has cast men into prison without trial. Lo! I will take the part of these Celestials, even the Head Sinters of the Goins and the Topi Kongs,

21. And I will show unto them that they have been badly treated and that there is no need that this money be paid. And I will plead for them, that the right may prevail,

22. For he was a good man, and cared not for lucre, which is called filthy, even unto this day, so that no man with clean hands and a pure heart will touch it.

23. So he departed,

24. And the hearts of the people went with him, for the men of Jonbool were just, so that even though their houses and goods were destroyed, they would not that men be punished without a hearing before the Judges.

25. For the men of Jonbool were not without blemish in the Far East, for they had boned much land,

26. "Now to bone, being interpreted, is to rob, and to bone land is in the language of the men of Jonbool to Colonize, but in the language of the men of the Far West, even in the land of Bruthir Jonathan, though they be of the same tongue, is to annex.',

27. And there was much impatience that the end of this thing might be heard.

CHAPTER VI.

1. And the Chief Ruler, after a short absence, returned to Singapura.

2. Now when he was come nigh unto the coast, a mighty

shadow came over that part of the island which is called Government Hill.

3. And the people were filled with amazement and ran about saying: Lo! it is a bright day, neither is there any cloud in the firmament. Whence then cometh this shadow?

4. But some of the people who were standing by the river-side looked toward the flag-staff, and beheld an immense flag, of such a size as had never before been seen in those parts, and it cast a great shadow upon the earth.

5. And upon the flag was a large crown.

6. Now it was not lawful that any but the royal family should have a crown upon a flag.

7. So the news was noised abroad that the good Victoria, even the Queen of the land of Jonbool, or Andrew Johnson, the President of the land of Unculsam, had arrove.

8. And there was much rejoicing.

9. And the people flocked from their houses that they might greet Victoria or Andrew as they approached.

10. Now when the ship which had the same flag as that on the flag-staff came nigh unto land a boat was lowered, and a man descended into it, and was rowed by the sailors towards the shore.

11. And when the people saw that it was a man, they said among themselves, Lo! this is not Victoria; it is Andrew, even Andy of the land of Unculsam,

12. But as he came nigh, they discovered that it was the Chief Ruler.

13. And they were one and all filled with amazement, and said: It cannot be a Crown that we saw on the flag: Verily it must have been a Bull, even an Irish Bull.

14. And they look fixedly at the flag.

15. And some among them squinted through tubes, which are called Spy-glasses.

16. But they all agreed that it was a Crown.

17. Then said Snuffers, whose surname was John, and who was a wise man among the people: I say unto you that ye are all sold, every man except myself.

18. For it was given unto me for a long time to know that our Chief Ruler was of the Royal family.

19. Now ye know wherefore it was that he ordered a throne, and moreover why he takes upon himself such power, even authority greater than the Queen.

20. For it is written that in this generation a man knoweth

more than his mother, and if he know more, why shall he not *do* more.

21.   And our Prince came among us in disguise that he might see whether we were loyal and worthy subjects of Victoria, our Queen.

22.   Now when the people heard these things they were filled with fear, and their limbs quaked, like unto the limbs of them with the ague.

23.   Then arose their Philosopher, and turning up his nose, spake unto the people : Fear not : Perhaps even now he is not of the Royal blood, but is playing a *goak*.

24.   Now *goak* in the language of the men of Unculsam, is being interpreted into the tongue of the men of Jonbool, a sell.

25.   And the people, after making enquiry in many places, knew that it was even as the Philosopher had said.

26.   And they were indignant in that they had been sold.

CHAPTER VII.

1.   Now there was a certain profession among the people which was called Banking, and the men of that calling were Bankers.

2.   And there was one among their number which was noted for the gentleness of his demeanor, and for his Christianity.

3.   But his gentle heart was also filled with indignation like unto the hearts of the others.

4.   And he said unto himself : Has not the Chief Ruler sold me ; why then shall I not sell the Chief Ruler ?

5.   Is it not written, that ye shall do unto others even as others do unto you.

6.   So he cast about how he should encompass his design.

7.   And as he sought, his eyes fell upon a piece of paper, which had come from the house of the Chief Ruler.

8.   And there was no writing upon it.

9.   So he sat himself down and wrote unto a merchant that the Chief Ruler would like to have the advice of this merchant at all times and on all subjects, even in the Council Chamber.

10.   For it is written, that two heads are better than one.

11.   And he sent the parchment unto the merchant.

12.   Now when the merchant saw it, he was pleased, for he said : Our Chief Ruler does many things which are not right in

mine eyes.   Now therefore I will try if I can turn him from his evil ways.

13.   And he wrote unto the Chief Ruler, and promised that he would advise him, even as much as he wished.

14.   And he sent this parchment unto the Chief Ruler.

15.   So when the Ruler saw what was done in his name he was wroth, and would have given the Banker over to the tormentors, but they had sloped.

16.   And the merchant was wroth, but he was a good man, and a gracious, and his bowels of compassion were open, and he frankly forgave the Banker.

17.   Yet his frame was weiry,* and he could have punished the Banker had it seemed good unto him to do so.

18.   And moreover, the merchant besought the Chief Ruler, that he would cause no noise in the matter.

19.   But the Chief Ruler was a man of war, and had no bowels of compassion.

20.   So he caused a parchment to be written to the Banker, and he reviled him therein, calling him a *forger*, which being interpreted means a *thief*.

21.   Then the people saw that the Chief Ruler did not appreciate *goaks*.

CHAPTER VIII.

1.   Now it was a custom of the people of Singapura, that they should choose from among their number three men who were noted for their industry and for their wisdom.

2.   And they were called Municipal Commissioners, because that they were commissioned by the people to make contracts with the men of the East for works of necessity in the town.

3.   And it was among their duties to see that the roads were kept clean, and that drains were built to carry off the filth, so that no sickness might come among the people by reason of evil vapors and stenches arising from the ditches by the roadside.

4.   Moreover, they made themselves responsible that the men of the East who did these things should receive just payment.

5.   And they also did contract for the building of public houses,

and for these and for the drains a vast number of bricks were required.

6. And the former Ruler had always given bricks unto them, even bricks make by the Government Officials called Convicts, which were cheaper and better than other bricks.

7. So it was the custom of the Municipals to enter into contracts for bricks likewise.

8. Now when the Chief Ruler heard these things, he was sore vexed, for he said within himself: These men have too much authority in the land: Verily, I will show unto them that this is a one man Government.

9 Therefore sent he word unto them, saying: Ye shall make no more contracts of any nature, and ye shall also refuse to fulfil those which ye have already made.

10. And nary a brick which ye have promised from my clay-pits shall be delivered unto you.

11. Moreover, ye shall return unto me every brick that is in the hands of the builders.

12. For I have need of them to build my palace upon the hill which is called Prinseps, which being interpreted, meaneth 'the hill of the Prince.'

13. Now when the Municipal Council heard these words, great fear came upon them, and they consulted among themselves what they should do.

14. And one of them which was a Lawyer rose up, and he placed his finger upon his nose, even upon the side of his nose, and said, Walker.

15. Now when a man places his finger upon his nose, and says, Walker, it meaneth, Not as I nose on.

16. Then arose another of the Councillors, and he spake unto the Council, saying:

17. Brethren, how is it possible for us that we can do this thing that is demanded of us.

18. Verily, if we break these contracts which we have made, shall not those men with whom we have bargained, take us into the Court before the Judges, and shall not damages be awarded unto them.

19. Therefore it is not possible that we break our engagements.

20. Then arose another member, and opened his mouth and spake, saying: Brethren, why should we vex ourselves? Lo, we will possess our souls in peace, and it shall be that when we be taken before the Judges, and damages shall be given against us,

we will bring witness that we would have fulfilled our contracts, but that the Governor prevented us, and we will bring an action against the Ruler.

21.   And they asked the Lawyer if this might be done.

22.   And the Lawyer, answering, said unto them: Yea, verily, that can we do, and he charged his brethren that they should pay unto him five Mexicans, even five shekels of silver each for the advice.

23.   And each man gave unto him a chit for five shekels, but charged him that he should not say anything more.

24.   Then the spirit of the Municipal Council arose, and the members did likewise.

CHAPTER IX.

1.   Now in the building which was called the Town Hall, the people had placed paintings and images of the Rulers who had governed Singapura aforetime, and who were beloved by the people.

2.   Moreover, the payment for these was from the pockets of the people and of their own free-will.

3.   And the Governor, wandering about the Town Hall, seeking what he might devour, did cast his eyes upon the paintings and images.

4.   And immediately his soul was filled with a great longing for them.

5.   And he said within himself, Lo! these things would beautify the walls of my palace, and I must demand of the Municipal Commissioners that they deliver them up to me.

6.   For the Municipals were also Custodians of the property of the people.

7.   And he sent word unto the Municipals that they should send them to him.

8.   And the Municipals told unto the people what had been demanded.

9.   Then the people were sore vexed, and said: What manner of Ruler is this that he should do these things. Verily he will come into our houses, and possess himself of whatsoever seemeth good in his eyes.

10.   For are not these paintings and images our own, even as much as the property under the roofs of our houses.

11. And they instructed the Municipals that they should be firm, and they should not be trodden down.

12. And immediately the spirit Bak Bone entered into the Municipal Commissioners, and they could not be bent.

CHAPTER X.

1. And when the Governor saw that the spirit Bak Bone had entered into the Municipal Commissioners, and that his arguments were of no avail, he sought how he could circumvent them.

2. For he wished greatly to obtain the paintings.

3. And he called unto him one of his evil counsellors (which being interpreted is Legislative Councillors,) whose surname was Thomas, and whose fame was so great that he was called the Queen's Counsel.

4. [For it was a custom in the land of Jonbool, to call men of repute who wrought in gold, Queen's Jewellers; and men who wrought in hair, Queen's Barbers: and those who were cunning in sausage meat, Queen's Butchers; and to judge by the number of the Queen's Counsel, she must have been before the Judges ofttime.]

5. And the Governor said unto Thomas: Tell me, I pray thee, how I may flank these Municipals.

6. Now to flank, in the language of the men of Unculsam, is to strike behind the ear, when the enemy is too scientific or possessed of too much firmness to allow of being prevailed over at the front.

7. So he sought to strike the Municipals behind the ear.

8. And Thomas answered and said: Master, make first a suggestion, that I may not disagree with thee.

9. Then said the Governor: Thou hast spoken well: Lo these Municipals are possessed of the spirit Bak Bone, and they will not give unto me the paintings which I desire, and which are in the building called the Town Hall.

10. Verily, I will wait until the Municipal Commissioners shall have adjourned, and I will possess myself of the keys of the Town Hall, and will fasten up the paintings and images contained therein.

11. And I will claim the Town Hall and all that therein is.

12. Now when the Chief Ruler had ceased speaking, Thomas being permitted of the Governor, opened his mouth, and spake, answering;

13. Not so Master, lest by that means you lose the painting of

Col. Cavenagh which is even now on the road.

14. Tarry until that also is placed in the Hall of the People, and then shall you be able to annex the whole.

15. And the Chief Ruler, after that Thomas had spoken, waxed exceeding wroth, and his cheeks were puffed out with rage.

16. Then spake he unto Thomas, saying: How is it that you call this the Hall of the People.

17. And Thomas answered mildly; I called it the Hall of the People in that the people paid for it.

18. And the payment for it was made of their own free will, and not by taxes.

19. Nevertheless, since the name appeareth not good unto my master, I will call it the Castle of *St George* for ever more.

20. When the Ruler heard this he was mollified, for the name received favor in his eyes, for he himself was called *Saint*, and his front name was *George*, though some mischievous ones did call him *Old Harry.* ✗

21. Nevertheless, he desired to be more assured, and he spake on after this wise:

22 But have not the people given over the Castle of *St. George* to the Municipals, and can I not claim all that is in the hands of the Municipals.

23. Then Thomas answering, said; I pray my Master that he be not angry, but I am a Lawyer, therefore must I tell the truth.

24. And the Governor bit his nether lip till the blood gushed out: And the Royal blood remains on the garment which is not mentionable till this day as a testimony unto these words.

25. And in a low voice he spake, saying: Thomas, say on.

26. Then Thomas being emboldened said: Master, the people have not given over the Castle of *St. George* to the Municipals; neither have they vested any right of possession in them; only as a Committee for the care of the Castle have they bespoken them. Therefore have you no right to it except such as might gives.

27. And when the Ruler heard this, he was vexed as with an evil spirit, and would not listen to the advice of his Counsellors, though they were evil, for the evil in them was not enough for his possessed spirit.

28. And he sat him down, and wrote at once that the Castle of St. George should be delivered up to him, and all that it contained.

29. Moreover, he ordered the painting of Cavenagh the Good to be given up to him so soon as it should arrive.

30. But he told the Municipals that they might reimburse the

people from the Treasury for the cost of the painting.

31. But the people were stupid and could not see it, for they reasoned among themselves after this wise :

32. Is not the Treasury our pockets, and have we not paid once for the painting : Now he does wish that we should pay again.

33. And a certain Banker held the talents of silver which had been given by the people for the payment of the picture.

34. And the number of the talents were three hundred, eighty and six.

35. And when he heard this thing, he buried these talents in the earth ;

36. Lest, he said, the Ruler get both paintings and money.

37. And the people applauded this act of the Banker.

38. But of the Ruler they said with one accord : Surely this *is* the *Old Harry*.

CHAPTER XI.

1. And it came to pass that when these things came to the ears of the Queen of the land of Jonbool, she was much troubled.

2. And she sent for her chief counsellor who was called Darby, and said unto him.

3. Lo ! we have sent unto our people of Singapura a ruler for whom there is no respect.—Tell me now what shall we do that they may show reverence unto him

4. And Darby scratched his head, for it was a hard problem which was proposed unto him.

5 And suddenly there shone a bright light in his countenance, for an idea had occured unto him, even a solution of this difficult problem.

6. And he opened his mouth, and spake unto the Queen, saying : I have hit it.

7. And she answered : Wherein ?

8. Then said Darby : Did not my gracious Queen offer unto one Field, of the land of Unculsam, whose surname is Cyrus, that he should be a knight of the land of Jonbool, because that he had put down much iron wire at the bottom of the sea, between our own land and the land of Unculsam :

9. Behold now the honor was refused by Cyrus, because that the

custom is not known in his own country, for the Chief Ruler of the
land of Unculsam is called Mister only, and none is acknowledged
above him.

10.   And had Cyrus accepted this honor, he would have been
laughed to scorn, because of the ignorance of the Yengeese, even
the men of the land of Unculsam.

11.   And so it happens that there be a vacancy among the knights.

12.   Peradventure, if our good Queen make the Chief Ruler of
Singapura a knight in the place of Cyrus, the man of wire, then
shall the people shew reverence unto him.

13.   So the Chief Ruler was made a knight, and the people of
Singapura called him Knight of the Iron Cross, because that he was
made from or crossed with the man of Iron Wire, even Cyrus of
the Yengeese.

14.   And when the news came unto the people, they said among
themselves—Surely our good Queen knows not of this man's doings.

CHAPTER XII.

1.   Now after the Chief Ruler was *benighted* by the Queen, he
did wax exceeding large, even larger than before.

2.   And he did question within himself how he might obtain
more absolute power over his people.

3.   And he consulted with some of his evil counsellors,

4.   Then came Thomas, one of the Council, unto him in secret,
and said unto him; Master, I believe that it is possible for me to
fulfil thy desires.

5.   Nevertheless, the matter must be accomplished with great
caution, lest my brethren of the council should smell a rat.

6   [Now to smell a rat, being interpreted, is to suspect that a
thing is not according to Cocker.]

7.   And it shall be in this wise.

8.   That thou shalt take unto thyself the power of the Judges
of the Supreme Court.

9.   And it shall come to pass that when thou desirest to make a
decision different from that of the Judges, that thou canst do so, and
no man shall say thee nay.

10.   Then shall thy subjects fall down before thee, for they will
fear thy power, and will say among themselves; Lo! this man is as
mighty as Theodore, even Theodore the King of the Abyssinians.

11. [Now the Judge of the Supreme Court whose surname was Peter was absent from the Country for a season.] ✗

12. And the Governor said unto Thomas, Lo! is not Peter absent from the Settlement—Wherefore then should we use such caution.

13. Then Thomas answering, said : Because some of the Council may think within themselves that thou desirest to grasp all the power in thine own hands.

14. Then said the Chief Ruler ; Be it even as thou wilt.

15. When the next morning was come, the Council of the people were summoned, and a parchment was placed before them.

16. And on the parchment was written that the Chief Ruler should appoint the Judge, even such a man as he pleased.

17. Now this was written that the ends of Thomas and the Chief Ruler might be encompassed.

18. For it was not deemed good in the eyes of Thomas that he should speak at once what the Chief Ruler desired, but rather that he should imitate Tahli Rand, the same of whom it is written that he used language to conceal his meaning.

19. For Thomas knew in his heart that when this power should be given to the Chief Ruler, it would encompass all his designs.

20. For could not the Chief Ruler appoint that man who should be after his own heart, and who would be his mouth-piece.

21. And was not Thomas himself after his own heart.

22. And was he not learned in the law, and might not he be appointed of St. George to be the Judge.

23. But when the parchment was read, there arose a certain learned Doctor of the Physic, whose name was Littlerubbut, even the brother of Littlejohn who was the companion of Hood whose surname was Robin.

24. And he smelt a rat and did speak against the parchment.

25. Then arose a Centurion even the Captain of the Volunteers, and Tummusskot who were members of the Council, and they did support Littlerubbut.

26. And there was great confusion.

27. Then said the Chief Ruler, Lo! it is not I who ask this thing, but another man who told me to do it, even the Sekreterry of Stait.

28. And a certain Kling, which is of a black race, who run about naked, and speak in a strange tongue, was standing at the door of the Council Chamber.

29. And he opened his mouth and spoke after the manner of his people saying, *Arung gutheree a.*

30. And the language was new unto the Chief Ruler.

31. Moreover he thought it was one of the Council who thus spake.

32. And he was affrighted, and believed that the curse of Babel was descending upon him and his Council.

33. And he broke up the Council in haste.

CHAPTER XIII.

1. Now Tummusskot and Littlerubbut and he who was the Captain of the Volunteers, were of the members of the Council who were non-official.

2. And, as has been said aforetime, the officials were those that fished all they could out of the country, but the non-officials were those that fished not, but who were called honorable, whether they were or not.

3. And it pleased them.

4. For whether they walketh uprightly with clean hands and a pure heart, or whether they lifted up their souls to vanity and swore deceitfully, were they alike called honorable.

5. So they thought their sins were overlooked, and that they might be admitted of St. Peter without being crossquestioned like unto other men.

6. But on this occasion did they act honorably.

7. And when the people heard what had been proposed by the Chief Ruler they were sick at heart, and said: Verily, the evil spirit has not yet been cast out.

8. But the doings of the non-officials were applauded.

9. And the people gathered together, and supported the action of the non-officials.

10. And when it came unto the ears of the Chief Ruler that such a stir was made among the people, he called unto him Thomas, and said unto him : Why hast thou led me to do this deed.

11. Lo ! the people are again aroused against me ; yea, even as one man do they upbraid me.

12. And Thomas answering said : Lo ! it is but a murmur even as a sighing of the wind on the house-tops, but hath no substance.

13. And thou shalt see that a few feasts will dispel it.

14. For man thinketh not evil upon a full belly toward him that filleth it.

15. Make therefore a feast, and bid all them who have cried against thee that they come unto it.

16. And there is a certain man who is a dealer in piece goods, who thought that he should be called honorable, though he is not; and his heart is sore in that he is not bidden to the Council.

17. And he is a *young* man, and one of the chief against thee.

18. Let him I pray thee be *boosted*, into the Council.

19. Now to be *boosted* is in the language of the Yengeese to be exalted.

20. But the Chief Ruler answering, said: Is it not written that he who exalteth himself shall be abased, and does not this man exalt himself—Yes, even in his nose doth his exaltation appear. Therefore, I will not do this thing, but I will give a feast even as thou advisest.

21. Then Thomas scratching his head, said: Master I have an idea.

22. And the Chief Ruler answered : Speak it then quickly, lest it depart from thee.

23. And Thomas answered, saying: Is it not true that the people murmur because thou desirest to appoint Judges of the High Court.

24. And I say unto thee that it is because they fear that thou wilt appoint for a Judge, one who knows not the duties of his office, that they murmur against the degree.

25. Show unto them that they may look for a wise choice from thee.

26. And behold even now canst thou do this, for doth not the small court, even the Court of Requests lack a Judge.

27. Choose then a man well versed in law, and of experience and place him upon the bench.

28. And the Chief Ruler said unto him: Thou hast spoken well.

28. Then the Chief Ruler cast about him to find such an one.

29. And after looking through his kindred he could find no more brothers, so his choice fell upon his *Cousins.* ✗

30. And his Cousins was a writer in the office of him who cast up accounts for the Chief Ruler.

31. And he was cunning in figures, but knew nought about law.

32. Moreover though his Cousins were a good boy, he was still but a boy, and his years of discretion had not yet come unto him.

33. But his Cousins obeyed the word of the Chief Ruler, and he sat upon the bench.

34.   And when the people did speak unto him and call him Your Worship—as was the custom, he looked about him that he might find unto whom they spake.

35.   And finding no one, he discovered that it was even himself unto whom they called.

36.   And the Cousins of the Chief Ruler did pluck open the sleeve of his vestment, and did thrust his head therein, and did laugh, for he was but a boy and the title was new unto him.

37.   And when the people did hear that the Chief Ruler had used up his Brothers and appointed his Cousins, they said: Verily the appointments of this man are all in the family way.

38.   And they were more vexed than before.

CHAPTER XIV.

1.   Now the time approached when the Legislative Council should be closed for a season.

2.   And it was commanded by the Chief Ruler that preparation should be made for a great show, and that no expense should be spared, lest any man should say that his possessions were burdened with debt.

3.   And he ordered the members of the Council that were official, that they should buy all the gold lace that was in the shops of the dealers in tinsel, and should sew it about their necks and about their sleeves, and upon the hips of the garments that are called inexpressibles.

4.   Also he commanded that the coverings of their heads should be bound with tinsel and beads, and a feather placed therein.

5.   And his commands were obeyed, and the Officials did stand before him.

6.   Then said he unto them; Push out your stomachs, and gird your inexpressibles tightly about your loins, and hold up your heads that ye may look like unto men of war.

7.   And they did so.

8.   Then commanded he unto them that they should drill under the eye of the centurion for seven days, that they might not forget the dignity which their garments conferred upon them.

9.   So when the morning was come in which the Council should

be dissolved, the Chief Ruler did call together the captains of his armies and did send them with all their forces to the doors of the Council Chamber.

10. And there was a mighty host like unto the sands of the sea.

11. And about the first hour, it was noised abroad that the Chief Ruler was approaching.

12. And immediately the gun of the mighty fortresses of his dominions did belch forth flame and smoke, and the noise was like unto the thunders of Heaven, so that nought else could be heard:

13. And from the midst of the smoke came forth the Chief Ruler, and his looks were as unruffled as the face of a horsepond on a calm day, and no fear sat upon his brow.

14. Then said the people one to another, Lo! this man is a true soldier, for he walketh forth from the fire of these mighty guns, as though they were nought of which to be afraid.

15. And when he was come into the Council Chamber, he looked about him that he might find his throne, but it had been left behind.

16. So he did sit himself down upon a chair, and the air was rent with cheers at sight of this great condescension.

17. Then arose the Chief Ruler and spake unto the Council, and said! Nine months having passed, ye shall be released from labor.

18. But before ye depart from before my face, I would show all those things unto you which I have accomplished during that season.

19. For have I not reduced unto you the exorbitant demands of the propellers of hackney carriages that have so long *Klung* about you.

20. And have I not passed a law by which those who are not of our blood may be sent from among us.

21. Moreover, lest any man might say that I was unjust toward these foreigners, have I made the act which is called the Passenger Act that they may have comfort and health when they be deported from among us.

22. Also I have altered the boundary line of the possessions of the Rajah of Quedah. (Now to alter the boundary line is, as has been said aforetime, " to *colonise* in the language of the men of Jonbool, and in the tongue of the men of Unculsam to *annex*, and in the vulgar tongue to rob land.)

23. These things have I accomplished and much more, and I say unto ye that ye cannot have all these good things except by paying for them.

24. Give me therefore wherewith I may furnish my palace with floors of precious stone.

25. For it may not be said that your Chief Ruler treadeth upon the same common clay which is in the habitations of his subjects.

26. Therefore shall it be that every man shall lay by him in store of his substance to be delivered unto my taxgatherers.

27. And it shall come to pass if this be not found sufficient for me, that I will levy taxes upon merchants in foreign countries, who send merchandise unto us.

28. And this shall be greatly to the advantage of my people, for they shall then have many festivals, and shall not be overworked as in these days.

29. For the dealers in foreign countries will send little of their merchandise unto us when they learn of the taxes that shall be imposed upon them for so doing.

30. Thus my subjects having little to sell, may bask in the sun and climb greased poles all the year round.

31. Now at that time the people of the land climbed greased poles only upon the first day of the year,

32. And when they heard that each day should be like unto the first day of the year they did rejoice, and did give thanks unto the Chief Ruler.

CHAPTER XV.

1. Among the possessions of the good Queen Victoria which were presided over by Saint George, was Penang, which being interpreted is the Land of the Betelnuts.

2. And it was goodly place, and had much commerce with the Island of Singapore, and with the land of the men of Jonbool.

3. Now a mighty Company had been formed by some of the men of Jonbool, and they owned much ships, which puffed forth steam, and were propelled by huge pieces of iron which looked like unto the fins of fishes.

4. And the name of this Company was the Peanho. X

5. And their motto was a proud one, even *Quis Separabit!* which being interpreted into the language of the men of Unculsam (which is the same as the tongue of Jonbool, except that it is refined and revised) meaneth, "Who can bust us ?"

6. Now it was the custom of the ships of the Peanho, which did sail between the land of Jonbool and the Far East, that they should anchor at the shores of Penang to take the merchandise and the parchments of the Merchants.

7. Moreover it was written in their contract with the Queen of Jonbool that they should do thus.

8. And it came to pass that when the time of the contract drew near unto its end, the Peanho congregated together and said among themselves: Lo! is not our motto a true one, for who in these many years has been able to bust us?

9. And we have gathered together much wealth, and have increased the number of our ships, and our fame has spread abroad even to the uttermost parts of the Earth,

10. Now shall we make a new contract with the Queen, and we shall ask a much greater sum of money in return for carrying the parchments of her subjects than we have had aforetime.

11. Moreover we will not stop at the land of the Betelnut, even Penang.

12. And it shall be that when the men of Penang shall murmur at this, then shall the Queen give us more money, and we shall stop there as aforetime.

13. Moreover we will say that we be poor, and the cookers of accounts shall make it appear even as we say.

. 14. And when the Queen and her Councillors believe that we be poor, and that we have carried the merchandise and parchments of her subjects only to oblige the Queen, then shall they have compassion on us.

15. Then cooked they their accounts and brought them unto the Queen, and it came to pass even as they had said.

16. And the Company of the Peanho with one accord put their forefinger on the side of the nose, and said, Walker!!

17. For this is among the customs of the men of Jonbool when they have taken in their brother, or when they cannot themselves be taken in.

18. Now when the news of this thing came unto the ears of the men of Penang, they were sore troubled, and said among themselves: If this thing be true, and nothing be done for us, then we be ruined. And a loud cry went up from among them, because that they were cut off from their friends.

19. And they met together that they might petition the Queen that she should help them in their affliction.

20. But there were many thousand leagues between them and

their Queen, and they cast about to devise how they should send their parchments to Singapura in the meantime.

21.   For the Vessels of the Peanho did stop at Singapura, and would take their parchments and merchandise thence to their kinsmen in the land of Jonbool.

22.   And while they were talking, it remembered them that the Chief Ruler, had promised that the steamer which his subjects had bought for him, even the *Peiho*, should be of much use to them in time of need.

23.   Then felt they easy in their minds, for they felt assured that Saint George, the Chief Ruler, would send the *Peiho* to and fro between Penang and Singapura until they should hear from their Queen.

24.   Now the time approached for the departure of the Peanho from Singapura.

25.   And it was about this time that the *Peiho* came from Singapura, and the Merchants of Penang were glad when she came in sight, and said: Truly our Chief Ruler is a good man sometimes: now shall we be able to write unto our kinsfolk.

26.   Then ran they to their houses that they might write their parchments, and answer those that they had received from Singapura.

27.   And when they had written, they took their parchments in their hands, and went to the sea-side that they might send them in the *Peiho*.

28.   But when they had come unto the Sea-side, they found she had departed.

29.   So they rent their clothes with grief, yet murmured they not, for they said: Surely there must be some grievous matter of State to cause all this haste.

30.   And it came to pass that as soon as the *Peiho* had reached Singapura, the Chief Ruler rushed on board with his gun.

31.   For it had been arranged that the *Peiho* should return from Penang with all haste that the Chief Ruler and his followers might join in a hunt after wild beasts, in the territory of a neighbouring Prince.

32.   And the Chief Ruler took with him some of his Council, that he might not be blamed of them in the matter.

33.   Moreover, he said : Can I not say that it is necessary that I make merry with the neighbouring Rulers that there be peace and kind feeling between us.

34.   And this will be believed by the Queen, for she knows not

the simplicity of the Malay Princes.

35. So Saint George and his band of mighty hunters departed in the *Peiho*.

36. And they took with them another steamer called the *Rainbow*, that they might place therein the wild beasts and game that they should slay.

37. And when they came unto Johore, which lieth over against Singapura, they went down from their ships to the shore.

38. And every man took with him his gun, and his spear and his bowie knife.

39. Then they hunted.

40. And after that, they hunted some more.

41. And it came to pass that after several days had passed, one of the number who was of the household of the Governor, shot a mighty boar.

42. And when the news came unto the ears of Saint George, he went to gaze upon the boar.

43. And he lifted up his voice and praised him who had done the deed.

44. And he promised unto him that he should have the Star of India.

45. And while he thus spoke, a woman came running towards him, even a woman of the Toh-Peh-Kongs.

46. And she threw herself upon the body of the boar, and rent her clothes, crying, "Ambui! Ini babi sahya anam tahun sudah pihara," which being interpreted meaneth: Alas! this is my pig which I have kept for six years.

47. And when the Governor heard this he felt queer, and said unto his followers; Let us return unto our own country.

48. And straightway they returned in the *Peiho*.

49. But the body of the Pig came in the *Rainbow*.

50. And when the people of Penang did hear of these things they assembled themselves together, and said among themselves: "What manner of Governor is this that he should cut us off from our kinsfolk and waste our substance, that he and his household should shoot a tame pig."

CHAPTER XVI.

1. Now the Bill which was written by Thomas, even the Supreme Court Bill, did come before the Council.

2.   And it was opposed by the non-officials, even Tummuskot and Littlerubbut, and he who was the Captain of the Host.

3.   Also the Chief Justice did inveigh against it.

4.   But their voices were powerless.

5.   For when the Chief Ruler did say that it was his wish that any law should be passed, the officials or echoes did say likewise.

6.   And the Governor's echoes were to the non-officials even as three to one, so that the Governor and his echoes had their will in all things.

7.   Now one of the echoes was the Centurion of a regiment, who could say to his men, go and they went, and come and they came, and he was troubled with a conscience.

8.   And he had agreed with the non-officials, and had spoken against this Bill.

9.   But it came to pass that on the day when the vote was cast his place knew him not.

10.   So the Chief Ruler prevailed and the Bill was made law.

11.   Now when the people did see what was done of the Governor and his echoes, and that the power of the Chief Justice should be taken from him and usurped by the Governor, they were sore troubled.

12.   And some among them proposed that they should assemble the people together, that they might speak their minds openly on this thing.

13.   And about the third hour of the evening, the people did come together at the Town Hall.

14.   And it was filled even to overflowing.

15.   Then came Andrew, a money changer from the Temple, into the midst of the Assembly.

16.   And he opened his mouth and spake unto the people. And his speech was full of wisdom, and he shewed unto the people the iniquity and mischief of the new law.

17.   Moreover he did shew unto them the words which had been spoken aforetime, on this same matter by some among the great and wise men of the nation, even Darby and Grey.

18.   And all the Assembly with one accord, being pleased with the words of the money-changer, did shout—*Taurus y pro vobis*, which being interpreted, meaneth—" Bully for you."

19.   After Andrew had ceased speaking, arose Hatchsoon, he of whom it is written " that coming events cast their shadows before," and his words were those of eloquence, and did carry conviction to the people.

20. And many others did speak. And they were all of one mind.

21. Then made they a record of their speeches, and did send them to their Queen, even Victoria of the land of Jonbool.

22. And they prayed that she would give ear unto their prayer, and prevent these designs of the Chief Ruler.

CHAPTER XVII.

1. And it came to pass that the Captain of the *Malachites,* who also was Lieutenant to the Chief Ruler of Singapura did fall sick.

2. And when the physicians had consulted with one another, they agreed that he must depart from their coast, unto the land of his fathers even unto the country of the men of Jonbool.

3. Now one among their number who was a Gaul did say that he was possessed of a *foy gras*.

4. And it was acknowledged among the Doctors that when a man was afflicted with a *foy gras* he must seek for a cool clime.

5. So he departed.

6. And when he had gone from among his people, it was needful that the Chief Ruler should seek another Captain for the *Malachites*.

7. And it came to pass that while he was thus searching, he chanced to read the words of one of the Saints, even Paul.

8. And in the 12th letter of Paul unto the Romans, he came upon these words: Be kindly affectioned one to another with *brotherly* love; in *honour* preferring one another.

9. Then said the Chief Ruler unto himself: Lo! this is a place of *honour*, therefore will I prefer my Brother, as is commanded by this good man of old.

10. And straightway he appointed his Brother.

11. And there arose a murmur among the old lieutenants because of this act, for many of them had served among the natives of the land for many years, and were learned in their laws and customs and language, and they said: Shall this man be preferred before us who have borne the burden and heat of the day, while he has come amongst us at the eleventh hour. Lo! see what it is to be the kinsman of a great Ruler.

12. But the Chief Ruler answered, " Can I not do what I will with my own ?"

13. So he had his way even unto the seven and seventieth time.

CHAPTER XVIII.

1. Now in these days there came a mighty vessel unto the coast of St. George.

2. And she had on board many valiant fighting men, and much munition of war and many guns.

3. And her name was the *Perseus*.

4. Now for a long time she lay quietly in the harbour of Singapura.

5. There were among the crew many men which were called Paddees, which are from the land of Ouldarin.

6. And it was among their chief customs to play tunes on the heads of their friends with sticks, which were called Shillaleys.

7. And when their own heads were bruised, they dearly loved him who had injured them.

8. Moreover, if there were strength left unto them to do so, they turned the other side, as is commanded.

9. Therefore were they Christians.

10. And it came to pass that these men waxed tired of a life of peace, and said among themselves; Lo! We be spilin' for a fight. Whey tarry we here wid none to tread on the tails av oor coats.

11. And when the Captain of the *Perseus* did hear these words, he went unto the Chief Ruler, and said unto him,

12. The Paddees that be with me are vexed with the quietness of their life. Give me then some work for them.

13 And St. George answering said ; We be at peace with all our neighbours, therefore can I give you no battle to do.

14. Nevertheless tarry not here, but take thy vessel out to sea, lest they Paddees do come on shore and smite me and my subjects.

15. Lo ! I will give thee a letter to Sarahwhack who liveth not many days journey from this.

16. And he gave him the letter, and ordered him that he should depart from his coast for a season.

17. Now it was about this time that the Peanho should have come from home, with parchments from the kindred of them which dwelt in Singapura.

18. And it was the custom of the Peanho, when she came unto Singapura during the night, that she should fire a gun, and send up a rocket.

19. Now about the eleventh hour, when darkness covered the

face of the earth, and only wickedness stalked abroad, a gun was fired.

20. Then the people sprang from their beds, and ran to the sea-side.

21. And when they were come there, they saw the rocket.

22. And they looked steadfastly at it, and, some among their number said, ou-ou-ou as is the custom when a rocket goes up.

23. And while they gazed, the rocket burst into a cluster of stars. And one among the people who was an astronomer said unto them,

24. It is given unto me to read the stars, and I will tell ye what is written in these.

25. And he read : Lo ! I Stevens, depart.

26. Now this was the name of the Captain of the *Perseus*.

27. And it was desired of him that every one should know that he was going.

28. And when the people saw what was done unto them, they did bless Stevens.

29. · And they went their way homeward, and told their wives what had happened. And *they* blessed him likewise.

CHAPTER XIX.

1. Now it came to pass that the Chief Ruler waxed tired of his dull life.

2. So he cast about to find what would amuse him. And lo ! there was nothing.

3. Then said one of his Evil Counsellors unto him. Has not my master the yacht called the *Peiho*, and is it not at his command. Why then shall he trouble himself to seek distraction in this benighted place.

4. For are there not many lands that St. George, our Master, has not yet seen ?

5. And if it seemeth good unto our Master, what hinders that he shall visit the land of Siam, which is a land flowing with rice and ivory, whose King is wise and learned as Solomon of old. Moreover this King is famed in that he has given many rare and costly presents unto those who have visited him.

6. And the Chief Ruler answering said : All that thou hast spoken seemeth good unto me : nevertheless it is written in the laws of

Victoria : " Thou shalt not leave our possessions to visit those of any other ruler unless leave be granted unto thee so to do."

7.   Then answered the Counsellor, saying ; Lo ! shall this stand in the way of St. George, our master, who has given power unto himself, even power greater than that of Victoria herself.

8.   For can he not *suspend* the Chief Judge without trial. And can he not with a wave of his hand send all those who are not naturals out of his possessions ; Why then should the laws of a woman, who has less power than his own, stand in his way ?

9.   After these words, the Chief Ruler was puffed up, and he felt the dignity of his position.

10.   So he sent orders unto the Captain of the *Peiho* that he should make ready the vessel, that he might visit the land of Siam.

11.   And the Captain answered him saying ; Where shall I go for my coals that I may make steam, for I have no money, and it will cost above two thousand pieces of silver for these.

12.   Then answered the Chief Ruler ; I will tell unto the Keeper of the Treasury, that he shall furnish the dibs, and unto the Auditor, that it shall be written against the expenses which are called Special, and this charge shall come from the pockets of the people.

13.   So it was done even as he had commanded.

14.   And in the morning the Chief Ruler went on board the *Peiho*.

15.   And he took with him a Cockatoo, two monkeys, an Aide-de-Camp, and a parrot, besides other animals.

16.   And he sailed.

17.   And it came to pass that the third day after he had departed, a sudden darkness spread over the Earth in the midst of the day.

18.   And the people, alarmed, ran in every direction, shouting : What is this that has come upon us ?

19.   Lo ! it is early in the day, yet the darkness of night is about us.

20.   And some among them looked into the firmament of heaven and saw that the Sun had hidden his face with a black mask.

21.   And the people stood aghast and said one to another : Lo ! is the Sun hiding his face from us in sorrow at this new fault of the Chief Ruler.

22.   But one among them who was a wise man, answered them saying : It is not as ye think ! Ye fools ! ye have yet to learn the power of this man who can suspend Judges and deport Unnaturals. Know ye then that *power over the Sun* is given unto St. George

even like unto that of Joshua of old, and St. George has commanded that a portion of the Sun's light be hidden from you until his return.

23. Then said the people one unto another: What next?

CHAPTER XX.

1. Now about this time there arose a howl in the land of the Betelnuts, which made itself heard even unto the coast of Singapura.

2. And the people of Singapura did enquire the cause of the complaint.

3. And it was told unto them that the howl came from the mouths of the Sons of Confucius, which as has been said aforetime, were like unto other men, save that they had tails.

4. And they were a hard working and persevering race, and they had done more than any other people to increase the wealth of Singapura, and of the islands round about.

5. And it was found that in sixty days, more than two thousand of the Sons of Confucius had departed from the land.

6. And one among them being questioned, wherefore he had left the land of the Betelnuts, answered, saying: Lo! a new Ruler has come among us, and he has built himself a palace, and bought ships, and expended much treasure; and he has laid heavy taxes upon us that he might do all these things; and the land groans under these burdens.

7. Moreover we must pay ten pieces of silver, even ten Mexicans to be buried, after we be dead.

8. And if one of us dies, and ten Mexicans be not found in his pocket, then can his friends not follow to the tomb to pray for him, but he must be cast into utter darkness.

9. Moreover we be told that it is good for us to be made naturals, that we may have the protection of the Chief Ruler. But for this we must pay even five and twenty Mexicans.

10. And after that I was naturalized, I found that I had not money enough to bury myself.

11. And I feared for the welfare of my soul.

12. So I determined to depart out of the land.

13. And many others agreed to do likewise.

14. And it came to pass that when we were about to go forth, we did ask for a passport.

CHAPTER XXII.

CONCERNING GAM BEER. ✗

1. Now in the days of St. George there arose a cry in the land of Singapura, because of the dishonesty of some among the sons of Confucius.

2. For it was found that many of them did give thistles where they had bargained to give figs, and thorns after they received money for grapes.

3. Moreover they did mingle worthless stuff in much other of their merchandise.

4. And when they did sell injarubba, they did soak it in water, and did sell the water for the same price as the injarubba.

5. Nevertheless the merchants did receive it, and did pay the price that was asked, blaming no one.

6. Therefore were they thieves like unto the sons of Confucius.

7. For is it not written that those who *receive* are like unto the thieves themselves?

8. But there were among the merchants from Europe, some good men who looked upon the matter in this way.

9. And they met together at the Chamber of Comus, and did swear a solemn vow that they would no longer be thieves.

10. And they did write a petition unto St. George, the Chief Ruler, that he would make a law to punish these wicked men.

11. But they did ask that this law should punish only those who dealt wickedly in Gam Beer.

12. And this Gam Beer was in very much request in Singapura and did grow in Singapura and in the country round about.

13. But the merchants who were of the Chamber of Comus, did not ask protection against the wiles of the injarubba thieves.

14. For they said: It is only for forriners and men of the land of Unculsam that this merchandise is bought.

15. And the men of the land of Unculsam can take care of themselves.

16. So it was that the men of the Chamber of Comus did ask protection against the Gam Beer thieves alone.

17. Then was the law for the punishment of these wicked men written out by order of the Chief Ruler.

18. And it was sent unto the Council that it might be made law or refused, even as it pleased the Council.

19. And it came to pass that at the eleventh hour when this

wise law should have been passed, there arose one of the Council who did speak against it.

20. And he did bring forward a parchment that was signed by many of the merchants themselves.

21. And in the body of the parchment, these merchants did say that they had not been cheated enough.

22. And many of the Sons of Confucius had also signed it, for they said: We will act kindly unto these men, for do they not ask of us that we will still impose upon them?

23. And the parchment did also object to the law that was desired, in that it would interfere with *Free Trade*, which name was a war-cry among them.

24. For they said: Is it not *Free Trade* to impose upon our Brother in any manner that we can?

25. And is it not also *Free Trade* to place mud in our Opium, and to call it all Opium, and to receive the value of pure Opium if our Brother will believe our word?

26. And we will sell our brass for gold, and our chaff for wheat.

27. For is not this what is call *Free Trade* among us?

28. So when the Governor saw that they desired what they called *Free Trade*, he did say, Let them be cheated, since they desire it.

29. And one among the merchants who desired not this kind of *Free Trade*, did write long and wise letters in the papers.

30. And the front name of this merchant who was a Scott was *William*.

31. Therefore is he called Gam Beer *Bill* even unto this day.

32. And the Free Traders after that they had succeeded, went about seeking what they might devour.

CHAPTER XXIII.

1. Now the Chief Ruler did depart for a season unto the Island of the Betelnuts.

2. And all his household did go likewise.

3. Then the people of Singapura did rejoice, for they said one unto another: Now shall we have no more vexatious laws for the present, and peace and quietness shall again dwell among us.

4. But they reckoned without their host.

5. And it was in this wise.

6. A new Chief Priest had been sent unto the people of Singapura, to serve in the Temple.

7. And it came unto the ears of the Chief Priest that there was murmuring among much of the people because of the hour of the evening sacrifice.

8. For many of them did dwell in the houses of publicans.

9. And the time of the evening meal was at the seventh hour.

10. Moreover this was the hour which had been set apart for the evening sacrifice at the Temple.

11. So there were many good men who were absent from the Temple at this service, for otherwise would they have gone to their rest without nourishment.

12. And when the Chief Priest did see this thing, he was sore troubled.

13. And he said: Verily, my people shall not have this excuse before the Lord.

14. So he changed the time for the evening sacrifice unto the Sixth hour.

15. That so the people might pray without fasting save on those days for which fasting was ordained of the Church.

16. And the people was pleased because of this good deed.

17. But when the Chief Ruler did hear of it, he was wroth.

18. And he did revile the Chief Priest in that he had dared to change the hour of the evening sacrifice without permission of his Holiness,

19. For, he said: Am I not the head of the Church, as well as of the State?

20. And have I not ordered the evening feast on the Sabbath, at my palace, for the eighth hour?

21. And shall I alter my hour to please those of my minions who eat with publicans and sinners?

22. So he did send a messenger from the island of the Betelnuts.

23. And he did command that the hour of the evening sacrifice be again as aforetime.

24. Then was the Chief Priest amazed.

25. For he had been but a short season in the coasts of Singapura.

26. But the people were not amazed, for they said: Surely the evil spirit has entered into this man yet one more time: Can it not be cast out?

YE AUTHOUR REMONSTRATES AND MORALISES.

1.   Why are the men of Singapura stirred up because of the deeds of the Chief Ruler?

2.   And why are they disquieted because of his unjust doings?

3.   And who set them up to be the judges over him?

4.   His acts may be right in his own sight, yet wrong in the eyes of the congregation of the wicked.

5.   For if we go into the land of the Cannibals, shall we not find the men thereof eating their fellow-men?

6.   And though this be an abomination in the sight of men of different habits, yet be the Cannibals true to their instincts.

7.   Likewise is it with the Chief Ruler.

8.   Though all men speak of him that he doeth unwise things, yet verily do I believe that he is unto the manner born.

9.   Therefore acteth he according unto his instincts, and is not responsible unto his minions.

10.   And if he doeth right in his own eyes, are his acts not therefore righteous?

Copy of Petition lately presented to His Highness.

The undersigned, who dwell in the Hotels and Boarding Houses of Singapore, and who believe in the divine right of *Governors* to do all that which seemeth good unto them, do hereby implore the attention of His Mightiness to the utter want of respect shown by the Hotel Keepers to his evening service edict, and the necessities imposed thereby.

So far as your humble Petitioners' knowledge extends, the hour of dining has not been changed at any Hotel or lodging house to meet your Majesty's views with regard to the proper hour for evening prayer, and your Petitioners view this rebellious spirit of the Publicans with horror and disgust.

We therefore humbly beg that your Majesty will issue an order to these Publicans which cannot be misunderstood, threatening them with heavy penalties in case dinner is ready before eight o'clock on Sunday evening.

And your prostrate Petitioners will ever pray—*at any hour that your Majesty pleases.*

(Signed)

EXTINGUISHER

AND 347 OTHERS.

BOOK II.

CHAPTER I.

1 Now not long after this act of the Governor against the Chief Priest had been accomplished, he returned unto the Coast of Singapura.

2. And as he drew nigh unto the Coast, the *Peiho*, even the Steamer which conveyed him, did signal unto the shore.

3. Now this was about the Seventh hour of the morning.

4. And the signal did call the Goverment Officials unto the shore that they might receive his Highness.

5. Then obeyed the Officials the signal.

6. And immediately there were congregated on the shore, the Chief scribe, and the Captain of the host, the Water Carrier of his Highness and the Chief Cooker of accounts, beside many other Officials.

7. And after that they had remained there for a long period they began to feel anhungered and athirst, and they said one unto another, Lo! some evil must have befallen the *Peiho*, for she approacheth not the shore.

8. And they waited yet another hour until the sun was high in the heavens, and yet he came not.

9. Then began they to feel faint, for it was long past the hour for the morning repast.

10. Yet none among them departed, for they feared the anger of his Excellency.

11. Then began they to swear.

12. And about the hour of midday the vessel of the Chief Ruler came unto the shore.

13. And the Officials did rush on board the vessel, and did greet his Highness with words of affection.

14. Then said the chief scribe unto him, "I greet thee even as the bridegroom greets the bride, for now shall we feast. Lo! we have waited for thee since the seventh hour, and we be well nigh famished."

15. Then answered the Chief Ruler, and said unto him, "Get thee hence, thou wicked servant. Is not a sight of my face a sufficient recompense unto thee?

16. "It was with this belief that I have tarried so long in the

offing, for I might have arrived here three hours since, but I sailed outside that I might have my morning meal in peace."

17.   So the Chief Ruler offered unto the Officials no food, and after that they had begged a crust of bread and a glass of wine from the Chief of the Tanjong Pagar Dock, they departed murmuring each man unto his own home.

CHAPTER II.

1.   And it came to pass that one among the honorables who was a non-official desired to give up his place in the Council.

2.   And when this was made known unto the Chief Ruler, he called unto him Thomas, and said unto him:

; 3.   Lo! how can I make myself still stronger in the Council.

4.   For who shalt go out among the dealers in merchandise, and shalt choose from among them, one who will bind himself to act like unto the officials.

5.   And it shall be that when I say yea, he also shall say yea, and when I say nay, that shall he echo.

6   And thou shalt promise unto the man of thy choice that if he will do this thing, hearing with mine ears, seeing with mine eyes, and placing his nose in my hands that he may be led by it, that he shall be called honorable among his fellow-men.

7.   Then went Thomas out to do as he was commanded.

8.   And he called unto him William the Son of Adam, and offered to make him honourable if he would act according unto the words of the Chief Ruler.

9.   But when William heard that he was to sell his conscience, he would not.

10.   For he was a just man.

11.   Moreover he had invested largely in *Straits Produce.*

12.   Then went Thomas unto Gambier Bill.

13.   But neither would he sell himself for so small a price.

14.   Also unto one of the Pahdees, even one of those who come from the land of Ould Arin, did he offer the place. But Thomas was likewise rebuked of the Pahdee.

15.   Now when these things were noised abroad, the people were indignant, and said one unto another,

16.   " Behold the Chief Ruler thinketh to make even non-officials his echoes: Hath he not voice enough already, that he should

try to make some among us barter the independence of their thoughts, and even their truth for an empty title?"

17. And one among the people, who was of a weak understanding, said, Lo! is this not bribery and corruption?

18. But the multitude laughed him to scorn, for they said: Is it not written that "the King can do no wrong; and is it not the same with our Chief Ruler who hath power even greater than that of a King?"

19. Now when Thomas saw that none among the chief men would sell himself, he returned unto his master and told him all these things.

29. Then said the Chief Ruler,

21. Cast these wicked servants into outer darkness, and seek among the poor, the halt, the blind and the half-witted, for such an one as I desire.

22. And the people waited impatiently to see who among them was the half-witted one.

CHAPTER III.

1. Now the Chief Ruler was a generous man, for he stinted not of the money of his subjects.

2. And the people had given him one hundred thousand shekels of silver that he might build unto himself a palace.

3. And some of the Government Officials, even the Convicts, had labored upon it for many months, and it approached completion.

4. Then went the Chief Ruler to gaze upon the work, and, when he had looked, he said: Lo! I have used up the money that was given of my subjects and I have none wherewith to build a place for my oxen and asses.

5. Then called he his chief workman, even him who was called Makan Angin.

6. And he asked of him how much would be required for this work.

7. Then answered Makan Angin.—Peradventure I shall require forty thousand shekels of silver over and above what thy subjects have already given thee.

8. And when the Chief Ruler heard this, he called unto him the Council and said unto them.

9. Mine honorable subjects, I have called you into my presence that I might speak with you regarding my palace: And aforetime

I did tell you that one hundred thousand shekels of silver would pay its cost, and I did approximate very nearly unto the amount required, but the houses for my oxen and asses were forgotten of me.

10.   Now it shall be that you will grant more money for this good work, even forty thousand shekels of silver more than you have already given unto me.

11.   Then answered one of the Council, and said;   We thought that the asses were to live in the palace,—but since we are wrong, *and have no choice in the matter*, we give the money unto thee.

12.   Now it came to pass that news was sent to the Chief Ruler that a Juke, even the son of the good Queen Victoria, would arrive on the coast in the ninth month.

13.   And it was a custom of the country that when the Queen's Sons were received with magnificence by any of her Governors, that they should be rewarded.

14.   And the Chief Ruler wished that it might be so with him.

15.   And he said unto himself: Behold I will have my Palace finished in splendour before the coming of the Juke.

16.   Moreover I will command my subjects that they give me wherewithal I may make great feasts for his reception, that so I may be rewarded of the Queen.

17.   Then called he unto him the Chief workman, even Makan Angin, who was also a courtier and an echo, and had always been led by the nose.

18.   And the Chief Ruler commanded him, saying; See that my palace is finished by the ninth month, for at that time cometh the Queen's Son.

19.   But Makan Angin answered him saying; Master, it cannot be done.

20.   Then was the Chief Ruler wroth, and said : Behold now it shall be that if my palace be not finished at the time of the coming of the Juke, then shalt thou lose thy head.

21.   Then laughed Makan Angin in the sleeve of his garment, for he knew that it would be but a small loss.

22.   And immediately the Spirit, Bak Bone, entered into him and dwelt there.

23.   And he defied the Chief Ruler.

24.   Then was the Chief Ruler vexed in that he must for his honour cut off the head of his best echo,

25.   For until this time had Makan Angin no ideas but those of the Chief Ruler, and the words that he spoke unto his master had been soft and honeyed even like those of a maid unto her chosen.

CHAPTER IV.

1. Now in the sight of men, the paths of the Chief Ruler were righteous.

2. For he went unto the tabernacle twice on the Sabbath, to offer sacrifice.

3. Likewise also was it with Makan Angin.

4. And it was among their vows to the Lord on each Sabbath, that they would do no work on that day, neither themselves, nor their servants nor their maids, nor their oxen, nor their asses, nor anything that was under their control.

5. But it came to pass that a few days after the spirit Bak Bone had entered into Makan Angin, it again left him.

6. And he went unto the Chief Ruler and said unto him: "Lo! my master commanded of me that I should build up the Palace of Saint George ere the ninth month should be accomplished, that so the Juke might enter in at its gate, and dwell in splendour.

7. And were it in man's power to accomplish this work it should be done even as thou hast commanded.

8. Have pity then upon thy servant, and show unto him how he may do thy will.

9. Then answered the Chief Ruler unto him, saying: Thou hast spoken well, and thy head is saved unto thee. Hearken now unto my words.

10. Between this and the end of the ninth month there be many Sabbaths, even twenty and four.

11. Behold then it shall be that the artificers in wood and in stone, even those with whom thou hast contracted, shall work on those days.

12. But with the Convicts shall be no work, for they be Government Officials.

13. And it shall be that when the people see that the contractors alone do work that they shall say, They do it of their own will.—Behold! the Chief Ruler is in the straight path, and restraineth the Convicts from working on the Lord's day.

14. This shalt thou do, that so my palace may be finished for the reception of the Juke.

15. Then Makan Angin, willing to walk in the right path, if there were nothing unpleasant by the wayside, answered the Chief Ruler and said: But master, is it not commanded that we permit not even our *asses* to work on the Sabbath day!

16.   Then said the Chief Ruler, Verily, thou speakest gospel; therefore it shall be that *thou* shalt do no work on the Sabbath.

17.   Then sought Makan Angin for the Spirit, Bak Bone, but he found him not.

18.   So he went out from the Chief Ruler's presence, and did as he was commanded.

19.   But when the people saw what was done of the Chief Ruler, they said one unto another.—Behold now the Chief Ruler breaketh even the commandments of the Lord that so he may be glorified on earth and that the Juke may have "gas and bells" when he visiteth our coast.

CHAPTER V.

1.   Now on the 24th of the fifth month came the feast of the birth of the Queen of the Land of Jonbool.

2.   And it was customary on that day that the Rulers of all the possessions of the Queen should give a feast unto her people.

3.   And thus had it been aforetime in the island of Singapore.

4.   But the Chief Ruler had spent much wealth that he might build unto himself a palace and some beautiful ships which should be a pride unto the people.

5.   Moreover was he thrifty, and had asked of the Queen that she should give unto him more money for entertaining of her people in Singapura; for they drank much.

6.   And this increase had not yet been allowed unto him, so that his pay was not even much more than that given unto the President of the land of Unculsam.

7.   So he was wise and said unto himself: Is it not better that I should save the money for this feast, and do good with it in private?

8.   Perhaps also I may astonish my people by giving a cup to be run for by the horses of Singapura out of this money.

9.   This then will I do:

10.   As the day approach for the feast of the Queen, I will go on board my vessel of war and will sail unto the shores of Djawa, even unto the land of the Dutchman which floweth with schnapps and with A. V. H.

11.   And when I be come unto the coast, and it be known that one of the Rulers of the Queen of Jonbool approaches, then shall it be that the mighty guns shall belch forth fire and smoke, and all

the men of war, both horse and foot, shall come out to greet me.

12. Then shall St. George and his power be known of the Dutchmen.

13. And I shall be waited upon by their Chief Ruler, and great honor shall be done unto me.

14. For have I not received my guests in this manner, even the Chief Ruler of Manila, and the Admirals of the French and the Austrians and the Americans?

15. And did I not invite the Austrian Admiral unto a feast, unto which he would have come had it not been for that "sunstroke," whereby he was forced to send a boy in his stead?

16. Thus then shall St. George gain honor among the nations about him, and save money for the races.

17. Then set he about to prepare that he might make much display among the Dutchmen.

18. And he called unto him the Captain of one of the Queen's ships of war, and demanded of him that he should make ready his vessel, and accompany the *Peiho* unto Djawa.

19. And the name of the war ship of the Queen was the *Rinaldo.*

20. Then the Captain of the *Rinaldo* answered him saying: It is not of my duties to do this thing, therefore must I refuse you.

21. Then spoke the Chief Ruler and said: It is among thy orders that thou CONVOY the Chief Ruler of a province whithersoever he may desire thee:

22. But the Captain said: If an O were an E, then wouldest thou be right, but the order of the Queen readest not CONVOY but CONVEY.

23. Then was the Chief Ruler vexed in that he could not proceed in two ships.

24. For his importance was too great to be held in one ship.

25. Nevertheless he bowed to necessity and the Captain, for he remembered him of the cost of the feast.

26. Yet tried he still another time, Saying: Thou art but a Captain, *Rinaldo*, and can I not command thee, seeing that I fly an Admiral's pennant at the mast head of my yacht?

27. But *Rinaldo*, knowing his duty, answered him saying: Assuredly thou fliest an Admiral's pennant at the mast head of thy *Peiho*, yet if I did my duty I should proceed on board and tear down thy flag, for thou hast no right to it.

28. Moreover the judges should mulct thee in five hundred shekels sterling.

29.   And *Rinaldo* showed unto the Chief Ruler that it was even as he said.

30.   Then was the Chief Ruler vexed as with a devil, and said within himself: Lo! I must proceed with but one vessel, and when I approach the coast of the Dutchman, and he perceiveth that I have but one ship, peradventure he will not receive me with the pomp which I deserve.

31.   Then cast he about to see how he might increase his importance.

32.   And suddenly a bright light shone in on his mind, and he thought within himself: Have I not the power to appoint the Judges of the Court?—Now therefore will I make myself the Chief Justice also, and will go among the Dutchmen even as two great men.

(And he *was two, for he was a man beside himself.*) *

33.   And I will demand the shillelah, even his mace of office of the Chief Justice that I may bear it with me to Djawa.

34.   Then sent he to the Chief Justice and demanded the stick.

35.   But the Chief Justice being of the land of Ould Arin, which love their sticks, would not surrender it.

36.   Then the Chief Ruler willing to appease the Chief Justice, sent unto him two small sticks with silver tops, and wrote unto him:

37.   Take thou these two small sticks and give unto me thy big stick of office, and all shall be friendly between us.

38.   But the Judge would not.

39.   Then waxed the Chief Ruler wroth for he dared not take the mace of the Court by force.

40.   And he said unto his counsellors: Look now on the evil of the independence of the Judges if it be granted unto them.

41.   Then the Chief Ruler was saddened, and said unto himself: Lo! I must proceed in one ship and as one man only. Nevertheless I will order much powder on the ship of war that much noise may be made.

42.   And he prepared himself and his followers for the voyage.

43.   And when he was ready, he went unto the philosopher of the period, even unto *Extinguisher*, and asked of him a letter of introduction unto some of the people of Djawa.

44.   For the philosopher had dwelt there for a period.

45.   But he would not, for he said: I will not disappoint his vanity by letting his character be known of these strangers.

46.   Let them find him out for themselves.

* P. D.

CHAPTER VI.

1.   After these things were accomplished he departed unto the shores of Djawa.

2.   And when he did come unto the land, he was received with much show, even as he should have received those of station who had visited his own possession. .

3.   And a great feast was provided in his name, for the Dutchman are fond of their food, as the shape of their bodies prove unto men, for they carry much about with them.

4.   So the Chief Ruler received all the attention which he sought.

5.   And when a few days had elapsed after the feast, he called unto him the Clerk of the Council, and said unto him.

6.   What more shall I do, which can be noised abroad unto my credit?

7.   Then answered the Clerk, who was also the Chief Cook, as has been said aforetime;

8.   Lo! there be many of the Queen's subjects in the land: Give then unto them a reception, that they may all bow unto thee.

9.   Thus then shall it be known in Singapura that thou art respected out of thine own dominions.

10.   (For the Clerk of the Council said, Surely they know him not in this distant place, therefore will they show him respect)

11.   Then did the Chief Ruler cause it to be noised abroad that he would receive the subjects of his Queen on an appointed day.

12.   And when the hour approached, he repaired in state unto the room which had been prepared for an audience chamber.

13.   And after much time had elapsed, there entered the Captain of the *Peiho*, and the Chief Engineer of the vessel (even his own officers.)

14.   And after a longer period came a third man and one woman.

15.   Then said the Chief Ruler unto the Clerk of the Council:

16.   Surely thou hast made a mistake in the hour, for it cannot be that none other than these should make obeisance before me.

17.   But after much time had passed, and none more appeared, he said, Verily this climate is unhealthy.

18.   And the following day he departed into the wilderness.

19.   And after that he had hidden himself there for a period, he returned without noise unto his own possessions.

20.   And when he had come unto Singapura, he found that there was still more complaint against him.

21. For six letters had come for him during his absence, and it was thought of his servants that it would rebound to his honor if they were despatched unto him by a private vessel, instead of sending them among the letters of common men, for whom a vessel was provided.

22. Therefore had they sent unto him a private fire-ship with six letters.

23. And the cost unto the people of Singapura was more than one thousand pieces of silver, which was near unto two hundred pieces of silver for each epistle.

24. So the people complained bitterly, and there was little peace for St. George.

CHAPTER VII.

1. Now there was a certain merchant in Singapura, who was called the oldest inhabitant, for he had dwelt in the land for many years.

2. And he was noted for the many services that he had performed, and many high offices of trust had been conferred upon him by former rulers.

3. And among others was the office of Judge of the Small Court.

4. Moreover the duties of these offices were performed by him without recompense, and much of his time was devoted to them.

5. And it came to pass that a charge was made against certain black men of the land (who are naked save that they have a small piece of cloth about their loins), that they had forged the name of a dead man in a parchment, whereby the property that would have been given elsewhere was diverted unto themselves.

6. So these men were arrested by the officers of justice and brought before the Court.

7. And another Judge was sitting upon the bench.

8. And it came to pass that when the cause was heard that there was not sufficient evidence against these men.

9. Therefore they were released, and went their ways.

10. And after a few days had elapsed, there came unto the oldest inhabitant some new witnesses, who did swear against these men that they were guilty.

11. Moreover they did affirm that these wicked men would depart that they might enjoy the fruits of their wickedness without let or hindrance.

12. And when the Judge did hear these things; he saw that he

had no time to call upon the Magistrate who had released them aforetime.

13.   So he did order their arrest.

14.   And they were brought before the Court again a second time.

15.   And when the new witnesses were heard, the evidence was found to be sufficient to send them unto the high Court of Justice to be tried.

16.   And it came to pass that when the Chief Ruler did hear of these things he said unto himself; " Lo ! have I not the power to remove the Judge of the High Court. Now, therefore will I try first how it works with a Judge of the Small Court.

17.   Then sent he unto the Judge, even the oldest inhabitant, and did tell him that he had sinned grievously in that he had arrested his black brothers after that they had been released of another Magistrate.

18.   And the Chief Ruler commanded him in haughty words to explain unto him why he had done this deed, without taking counsel with the Judge who had emancipated his colored brethren.

19.   Then explained the good Judge his reasons for acting as he had done.

20.   But the Chief Ruler would not be satisfied.

21.   And he sent again a second time unto the Judge a more haughty letter than the first.

22.   And when the oldest inhabitant did see how he was treated by the Chief Ruler, he said unto himself:

23.   " Shall my hairs which have grown grey in the service of my county without recompense or reward, meet with no respect ?"

24.   And strightway he sent unto the Chief Ruler, and demanded that he should be released from those duties which he had performed for so many years.

25.   Thus did the good Queen Victoria lose a faithful servant.

26.   And when the people heard of this thing, they murmured and said one unto another :—" Thus is it with the Chief Ruler : He surroundeth himself with sycophants, who lick the dust from before him, but behind him they do curse."

27.   Moreover he knoweth not a good and true man when he falleth in with him."

28.   " And he thought that our oldest inhabitant, being but a *Reed*, could be bent, or shaken by his " wind."

29.   " Moreover he doth not even appreciate the services of our philosopher.

EXTINGUISHER."

CHAPTER VIII.

1.   And not long after the return of the Chief Ruler from the Coast of Djawa, he departed unto the land of the Betelnut.

2.   For it was among the allowances and pickings of the Chief Ruler and his satellites, that whenever they went abroad from Singapura they should be allowed a number of shekels each day, over and above the number that they were allowed by the Queen.

3.   And these were *called* travelling *expenses*.

4.   Therefore did the Chief Ruler and his favored satellites travel much.

5.   Now the time was fast approaching when the Queen's Son, even the Juke, should arrive at the land of the Betelnut and at Singapura

6.   And the people of both these places, were true and loyal subjects of the Queen, desired that they might do her honour through her son.

7.   Therefore met they together, and debated among themselves how they could best carry out their wishes.

8.   And it was decided among them that they should give unto the Juke a great feast, and that each man should give generously of his substance to this end.

9.   Moreover did the people agree among themselves that they should request the Chief Ruler, even as the representative (however poor) of the Queen, that he should preside at the feast.

10.   Therefore went unto him from the land of the Betelnut and from Singapura certain of the people who were chosen of their fellows because of their virtue.

11.   And when they had showed him all these things, the Chief Ruler gave answer that he would consider upon their wishes.

12.   Now these things were done in Singapura.

13.   And after some days were elapsed he departed from the coast.

14.   Yet unto that time answered he never a word:

15.   But departed for the coast of the land of the Betelnut taking with him Thomas, the Billmaker, and a sprained ankle.

16.   And he called Thomas unto him, and said: Thomas, my mind is troubled because of the loyal wishes of my subjects.

17.   For they have sent a deputation unto me, and have asked that I will preside at a feast prepared for the son of Victoria.

18.   And they desire to pay for this feast, each man out of his own pocket.

19. Now these were my intentions, save that I wished to take the payment for the feast out of the Treasury, which is in fact the pockets of the people, though it appeareth not so.

20. Thus should I have had the whole credit of the feast.

21. And when it should come unto the ears of Victoria, peradventure if the feast were costly even like unto the price of my palace:

22. Then might the Queen make me a peer in the land for the honour done unto her son, the Juke.

23. Tell me then Thomas, I pray thee, what can I do, that I may encompass my designs.

24. And Thomas answering, said: Master, I have an idea, which I trust may have favour in the eyes of my Lord.

25. And it shall be in this wise.

26. When my Master shall have come unto the land of the Betelnut, he shall call before him the people of the place, and shall say unto them;

27. My children, I think ye for your loyal expressions toward Victoria and for the kind offer of yourselves and the good people of Singapura to *assist me* in giving unto the son of the Queen, even the Juke, a reception that is fitted unto his position.

28. Moreover, I doubt not that I shall be able to do all that is meet unto the occasion.

29. And I shall not forget you.

30. Then the Chief Ruler pondered upon the speech of Thomas:

31. And it was good.

32. And when he had arrived at the land of the Betelnut, he spoke even as he was advised of Thomas, the Billmaker.

33. And when the people heard it they were amazed.

34. And they departed each man unto his own home crying Walker! Walker!

35. And they sent up a howl that reached even unto the skies.

CHAPTER IX.

1. And the Evil spirit that possessed the Chief Ruler would not be cast out:

2. But encompassed him more closely round about, and folded its black wings about his soul :

3. So that he saw not as other men saw, and his walk unto their eyes seemed "slantendicular."

4. For at this time came Jonah, called Daniel, one of the uncovenanted servants of the Queen, from the land of Victoria, where he had sojourned for a time, that he might become learned in the laws of the land :

5. That so he might administer them with justice.

6. For aforetime had he been a judge in the Courts of Singapura.

7. Now a judge is one who administereth justice with scales—over his *Eyes*.

8. For *all mankind* have their scales over their eyes —some by reason of love, some by reason of jealousy, others by reason of pride ; while there be some who are so covered with scales that they be called of their fellow men, scaly.

9. And of such was the Chief Ruler.

10. Now about the time when Jonah called Daniel (not he who was cast into the lions' den; neither he who passed through the whale) returned unto Singapura, there was a vacancy among the high officers of justice.

11. And it was expected of Daniel and of all the people, that the Chief Ruler would confer the dignity upon Daniel.

12. For he had served the Queen in the administration of the law for many years—even for more than twenty years had he served his Queen.

13. Moreover during his sojourn in the land of Victoria, had he perfected himself in the law, that so he might make black appear white, and white, black ; and right, wrong ; and wrong, right, after the manner of all great pleaders.

14. (And all mankind looked upon this as glorious, and applauded those who were successful in such deceit.

15. Thus had they their glory in *this* world, but were debarred from the happiness of the next.

16. For it is written that : It is easier for a camel to go through the eye of a needle, than for a lawyer to enter into the kingdom of Heaven.)

17. And Jonah, called Daniel, was a lawyer.

18. Then Daniel applied unto the Chief Ruler, that he might occupy the seat left vacant in the hall of justice.

19. But the Chief Ruler turned unto him a deaf ear, and would not.

20. But appointed another who was a good man, but of tender years, and who lacked the experience which was possessed of Daniel.

21. Then Daniel, being justly indignant, resented this act of St. George.

22. And he sent word unto St. George that he would no longer labour for the Queen, who could thus treat him through her servants; but that he would serve himself.

23. And straightway he did even as he said.

24. Thus did the Queen lose the oldest judge from her dominions, even as she had lost the oldest inhabitant, as has been told aforetime.

25. And the people sorrowed greatly, and enquired in their minds how they might cast out this evil spirit.

26. And one of the chosen asked of the Chief Ruler,

27. Why hast thou done this thing? Hast thou not cast out one who has borne the burden and heat of the day, and placed in the seat which of right was his, one who has entered the vineyard at the eleventh hour?

28. Then answered St. George, saying: Thou fool! is it not written that I may do what I will with mine own. And are not ye all my slaves?

29. Moreover this Daniel, though he be well versed in the ancient law of the land, yet knoweth he not the new ones of Singapura.

30. For have not I and Thomas, the Billmaker, laid hundreds of legislative eggs?

31. And hath not Thomas incubated, and hatched hundreds of amendments from these?

32. And Daniel knoweth nought of the omeletology of these new laws.

33. Moreover it would take him years to understand them.

34. For I, even I, and Thomas the Bill-maker, understand them not though we hatched them.

35. And I knew that if I appointed a man of much mind, that the study of these things would drive him mad.

36. Therefore did I have mercy upon Daniel, and did release him.

37. Now when the people heard these things, they were filled with joy.

38. For they said: There is still some good in St. George, for he displayeth a kind heart.

39. But all these things were seen clearly by

Thomas Braddell, Atty. Genl.

EXTINGUISHER.

CHAPTER X.

1. And even as was said aforetime, in the 2nd Chapter of the 2nd Book of the Chronicles, the people waited impatiently to see who among their number would accept of the title of honourable.

2. And after many days were accomplished, the Chief Ruler sent unto two of the people, and said unto them—Ye have aforetime refused the honour that I offered unto you.

3. Now have I received instructions from the land of our Queen, and it shall come to pass even as I now say unto you:

4. And it shall be in this wise: If ye accept not now the position which I offer unto you, then shall it be that I appoint two black men, even niggers, to fill these places.

5. And the names of these men are Perrianna Chitty and Veringapitty.

6. So shall there be an Honourable Veringapitty and an Honourable Perianna Chitty in the Council, making laws to govern ye.

7. And one of them, wishing to appease the Chief Ruler, said unto him :

8. But our Master does not remember that he is even now making laws against smells.

9. And it is well known of us all that even that which is now called the Bouquet d'Ord doth not emit a perfume like unto the incense from the bodies of these men.

10. Will our Master then take this incense even under his very nose.

11. Peradventure even these very sweet-savoured men shall vote against smells.

12. But the Chief Ruler said unto them : I will have them washed and perfumed by the Chief of the Waterworks even at the door of the Council Chamber.

13. And when they saw that the Chief Ruler would do even as he said, the spirit Bak Bone departed out of them :

14. And they became honourable.

15. And were appointed to fill the places of the two blacks.

16. And they thought within themselves that they had done a good deed toward their fellow men.

17. But it reminded the Philosopher of an incident that had once happened unto himself.

18. For once when journeying in the wilderness of the land of Unculsam, he was an hungered and athirst.

19. And he stopped by the wayside at a house wherein dwelt an old woman.

20. And she placed before him the food of the country, even baked beans.

21. And when he had eaten his fill, and returned thanks, he desired to depart

22. But she would not, but begged him that he would eat more.

23. And he answered her that he was filled, and could not.

24. Then prayed she but the more, saying: Fear not that thou takest away from my store, for whatever thou dost leave, I intended for the pigs.

25. Thus likened she him even unto her pigs.

26. Yet resisted he the widow's *cruise* and departed on *his own.*

27. Did not the Chief Ruler liken these two men unto his *pigs*, and told them that he would give what they left, unto them?

28. Yet saw they not the *stye* in his eye, and departed, rejoicing.

29. So *William*skot (even Gambier Bill) the brother of Tomskot—who was honourable before him—and William, the son of Adam,¥(not that one which killed Abel) were admitted into the Council.
(Vice Perrianna Chitty and Veringapitty)

30. And they were prayed for on every Sabbath day by the Chief Priest and the people in the temple, and daily in the wilderness by

EXTINGUISHER.

CHAPTER XI.

1. And it came to pass that when the building of the palace was accomplished, the Chief Ruler and his followers removed within its walls.

2. And he took with him his elephant and his flocks, his herds, his cockatoo and all that was his.

3. And after that he was sat down, he sent and called unto him Mustirattindint, and said unto him:

4. Raise up for me upon the roof of my palace a large staff from which I may display my banner.

* P. D.

5. And Mustirattindint said unto the Chief Ruler Would it not be better to plant a large staff in front of thy palace, as is the custom ?

6. But St. George cast upon him a withering glance, and said unto him :

7. Mustirattindint : hast thou ever visited the Queen at her Palace of Buckingham ?

8. And Mustirattindint said that he had not done so of late.

9. Then answered the Chief Ruler : This then accounteth for thine ignorance ; for when I visited the Queen, and was taken to view the Palace, I saw the staff for her banner upon the walls and it is meet that I have my palace arranged even like unto that of the Queen.

10. Then Mustirattindint, being overcome by the majesty of the presence, subsided, and answered never a word :

11. But went and did even as he was commanded.

12. And the Chief Ruler planted his banner upon the walls, even as it is in the Palace of Buckingham.

13. Moreover St. George had his own way in all things as aforetime, and his course was unchanged, for there were now none to dispute him.

14. For the time was drawing near when the Juke should visit the coast.

15. And many of the enemies of the Chief Ruler had turned their coats even unto the last sleeve, that so they might be in the good graces of St. George, and be made of importance in the pre-sence of the Juke.

16. (For when a man changes the side of his coat, it signifies that he changes his principles likewise.)

17. Moreover there was a great feast to be given by the Chief Ruler, and his opposers feared that they would be left in the cold.

18. Now when the Philosopher saw all these things, he thought within himself :

19. Shall I not likewise turn my coat and show myself unto the Chief Ruler that I may also sit with royalty ?

20. But the early principles of virtue that had been instilled into his heart, permitted not of it.

21. And he turned him unto his tub, and moralized upon the strange ways of the world.

CHAPTER XII.

1.   Now there was in Singapura a certain Club which was called the Tangleing Club, because that at the joyous dances and merry-makings held there many heart-strings had become entangled for life.

2.   And when the Chief Ruler had newly come to govern the land, the chief men of the Club, wishing to do him honour, had invited him to come to one of these merry-makings.

3.   But St. George, enwrapping himself in pompous dignity, had returned no answer to the Chief men.

4.   Therefore waxed they wroth.

5.   And they passed a law that he should be invited no more.

6.   And when the time drew nigh for the arrival of the Juke, it was made known that the son of the Queen was exceeding fond of the sports of the Club.

7.   And it was decided that he should be invited to join in them.

8.   And when this had come unto the ears of the Chief Ruler, he sent unto the chief men, desiring that he also might be invited.

9.   But the chief men, remembering them of the slight put upon the Club, would not.

10   And it came to pass that when the Juke had arrived, the Chief Ruler sent straightway unto him, and begged him that he would not enter the doors of the Tangleing Club.

11.   And the Juke, knowing nought of the matter, consented unto the request of St. George, and joined not with his own countrymen, who loved him much for his Mother's sake.

12.   But was led by one of the dragons of St. George unto a Club of foreigners, and disported himself there.

13.   Thus did the Chief Ruler again show the smallness of his mind, and drive another nail into his official coffin.

CHAPTER XIII.

1.   And there was a feast at the palace of the Chief Ruler, and all the subjects of the Queen who dwelt in the land of Singapura, were bidden unto it, that they might meet the Juke.

2.   And among the number of the guests, was Hatchsoon, the notable pleader.

3. [He it is, of whom it was written that his paths dropped fatness.]

4. And Hatchsoon went unto the Chief Dragon of St. George, whose surname was Pullow, and said unto him:

5. Why is this dissension between the Chief Ruler and the people?

6. It is not better that we dwell together in peace and amity?

7. Then answered the Chief Dragon saying: Ye have not bowed down before us, as ye must; and I say unto you that ye shall all go down on your marrowbones to us, before there shall be peace between the Chief Ruler and the people.

8. Then Hatchsoon, being incensed because of the rudeness of the speech of the Chief Dragon, answered him saying:

9. Peradventure *thou* art the Chief Ruler, and *thine* are the acts of which we complain, for such one would judge from the manner of thy speech.

10. Then said the Chief Dragon: Lo! in this matter 'tis even as thou sayest.

11. And when Hatchsoon reported these words unto divers of the people, they expressed no surprise:

12. For it was known of many of them that Pullow acted ofttime in the capacity of Governor, as well as Chief Cook, and that many of the unhappy dissensions had been caused by his acts and by reason of his evil counsels.

13. And it was remarked by many that the nose of St. George was fast increasing in length, for he had been led much by it.

CHAPTER XIV.

1. Now, in the land of Johore, that lieth over against Singapura, there dwelt a native King.

2. He it was to whom was given the noble order of the Star of India, that an exception might be made to prove the rule that this decoration was bestowed upon those who had achieved some glorious deed.

3. And after that the Juke had been feasted in Singapura, he was invited of the native King to visit his dominions.

4. Moreover, the King commanded that a mighty feast should be prepared, and that wild beasts should be procured to fight and rend each other before the Juke.

5. For such is the custom among these barbarians.

6. And the Chief Ruler, even St. George, with his dragon and his other evil counsellors, and all of the chief among the dealers in merchandise, were bidden to the feast.

7. And the hour set apart for the feast was the twelfth hour.

8. Now, as the twelfth hour drew nigh the guests which had been bidden unto the feast began to arrive.

9. And they were an hungered and athirst, for the journey was a long one, and the sun was fierce.

10. But when they came nigh unto the place of the feast, they found St. George, his dragon, and his evil cousellors, had well nigh finished the good things provided.

11. And they were wroth at such treatment.

12. Then one of them, who was a centurion, even the Captain of a hundred in the 75th, went unto the native King, and upbraided him, saying:

13. Why hast thou done this evil thing?

14. Didst thou not bid us to come to thy feast at the twelfth hour?

15. The time has not even yet arrived, and the food has well nigh disappeared.

16. Then answered the native King, and said unto the centurion:

17. Lo! the Chief Ruler said unto me, Thus must thou do, and I have done even as he commanded, for I look upon him as my master.

18. Then some among the people swore, for they saw that they were of less account than even the *stomach* of the Chief Ruler.

19. Thus did St. George, even within seven days, prevail upon the Juke and again upon the native King that they should show contempt toward the people of Singapura.

20. For his *own* discourtesy and snobishness was not sufficient unto him. ∧

21. And his selfishness and vanity knew no bounds.

22.. Thus again was another of the few remaining pegs driven into the coffin of the Chief Ruler.

23. And the people said one unto another: The name of the Chief Ruler is already inscribed upon his official coffin plate, and it needeth now but the date.

CHAPTER XV.

1.   And it came to pass on the day of the feast that was given by the native King that the Lieutenant of the Chief Ruler died.

2.   Now this Lieutenant was second only unto the Chief Ruler himself.

3.   And when St George was absent for a season, he ruled in his stead.

4.   And he was beloved much, for he had been many years among the people, and his heart was big with love, and gentleness.

5.   In so much that no man could say aught against him, for he had treated all with loving kindness.

6.   And when the news of the death of his Lieutenant came unto the ears of St. George, he was an attendance upon the Juke, in the midst of the sports provided by the native King.

7.   Yet stayed he not the sports.

8.   For he desired to show unto the Juke the majesty of St. George and the littleness of all other beings in the land.

9.   So he toadied unto the Juke, and went down continually on his marrowbones before him.

10.   For he thought within himself:

11.   If I impress the Juke with a sense of my majesty and power, and yet the readiness of that majesty to bend to him, mayhap his mother, when it is noised abroad, will raise me a step in rank.

12.   And it rested with the Chief Ruler to appoint the hour in which his great and good Lieutenant should be borne to his last resting place.

13.   And it came to pass, that when the sports in the land of Johore were ended, the Chief Ruler returned unto his own coast.

14.   And the people waited anxiously for his return, that the hour of the burial might be announced, that so they might accompany to the grave the body of one who was so justly beloved of them.

15.   Yet kept he the hour secret.

16.   Moreover he requested of the Chief of the Queen's forces, that the body might be laid in the grave without the Military honours that were due unto the departed.

17.   But the Commander of the forces would not consent.

18.   And when the hour for the burial drew nigh, the places of many of the near friends of the deceased among the mourners were vacant.

19. Therefore was the cause of this enquired.

20. And when the people found that the hour for the burial had not been noised abroad, and that the body had been taken to the grave, with a haste that was unusual and unnecessary, they were filled with indignation and cried aloud, saying:

21. Is it not enough that this man should insult the living?

22. Must he even show his pompous vanity and want of respect unto the dead?

23. So the Lieutenant of the Chief Ruler was gathered unto his Fathers, and his memory, even in his grave. was insulted by this man.

24. And it was felt more deeply of the people, inasmuch as the Juke himself had shewn respect unto the corpse of a poor and most humble servant of his but two days before.

25. And had followed the body on foot unto the grave.

26. Thus was given unto the people to perceive the difference between the acts of true, high-born Majesty, and the miserable vanity of a bird in false plumage.

CHAPTER XVI.

1. Now, after the death of the good Lieut. Governor, the Chief Ruler cast about him to see whom he should choose to fill this high place.

2. And his choice fell upon Kapitanshaw, even the Kapitan or chief man among the Malacchites.

3. Then was Kapitanshaw sent unto Singapura that he should fill the place of the loved departed one, and that he should govern in the place of the Chief Ruler during his absence.

4. For the Chief Ruler had gone to curry favour with the Juke.

5. Even unto the land of the Betelnut had he departed.

6. And when the Chief Ruler had made his choice, he sent his commands unto Kapitanshaw that he should depart at once for the coast of Singapura.

7. Moreover he said into him—There be few spacious dwellings there. Take thou, then, the house called Vonderhider, which was furnished for the retinue of the Juke, and dwell thou therein.

8. Then departed Kapitanshaw unto the land of Singapura.

9. And he found all even as the Chief Ruler had spoken.

10. And he went to dwell in the house called Vonderhider.

11. But the Chief Ruler remained for a long season in the land of the Betelnut, and in the province called Wellington, which is also of the Queen's dominions.

12. And he did much good there.

13. For it was noticed of the people that on whichever road he was to travel, all was made smooth.

14. So it came to pass that on these roads, holes which had existed for years were filled up, and all unevenesses removed :

15. Even as it *should* have been in the passage of Royalty.

16. Therefore did the people of the land of the Betelnut and the Province of Wellington rejoice.

17. And the Chief Ruler basked in the sunshine of their adulation :

18. But after a time, lest this sun should set, as it had always done aforetime in any region wherein he had long remained, he returned unto the coast of Singapura

19. And after St. George had returned a few days, his Dragon —(even Pullow who furnished him the marrowbones of merchants from the Square)—came unto him, and complained that he had not yet received his financial feed.

20 Then St. George who was enamoured of his Dragon, made out a bill in his name, and sent it unto Kapitanshaw that he should subscribe his name unto it—as was the custom—that so the treasurer might pay it.

21. But when it came unto Kapitanshaw, he said : Who is this man Pullow, that he should receive recompense for that he has not done. Had he done this duty for which payment is asked, he would have been in this same room with myself. Yet have I not seen him once.

22. Then whispered a timid servant in his ear; It is a favourite satellite of the Chief, and he nameth the Dragon unto the office that he may receive its recompense, without bearing its labour.

23. But Kapitanshaw was obtuse and saw it not in that light.

24. And he refused to sign the Bill because that it was unjust.

25. Then was the Chief Ruler wroth, yet could he not remove Kapitanshaw, lest he should cause trouble unto himself.

26. Therefore did he a small act, which was natural unto him.

27. For straightway he wrote unto Kapitanshaw, and demanded that he should leave the house where he dwelt, for the furniture belonged unto the Queen, and must be sold forthwith.

27. And when this was noised abroad one said—Is the Queen *hard up,* that she must sell this furniture so quickly ?

29. But one who was acquainted with the matter answered and said ; Not so, but that the Chief Ruler may pay the balance on the Steamer that is *not* coming out.

30. So was Kapitanshaw sent to look for a tent in the wilderness, with his flocks and his herds and all that was his.

31. And he found one belonging to a dealer in frozen water.

32. And he dwelt there.

33. Now, soon after, the Chief Ruler met the Philosopher eating the air of the morning.

34. And St. George said unto the Philosopher—Thou perceivest that I take the bull by the horns.

35. Then answered the Philosopher—I do twig even as thou sayest, yet if a weak man taketh hold of a strong bull's horns, and holdeth thereon without retreat, surely the man shall be tossed in the air to his injury?

36. —Then offered St. George to give odds to the Philosopher that he would hang on the horns, and get the best of the bull.

37. —But the Philo: would not bet, for he feared that all the money of the Treasury had been exhausted in Steamers and other extravagances.

38. Moreover, in a few days he was to leave the Coast for his own country, for the healers of the sick had ordered that he should bathe in the waters of the Mississippi.

39. And when the Chief Ruler heard that he was soon to depart, he went not unto the Philosopher's tub, which lay on Bukit Chermin, to thank him for the kind advice he had freely given unto him.

40. Nevertheless the Philosopher determined that he would write his Exodus in a farewell, trusting that the Chief Ruler might still find out that a true friend ofttime chideth.

EXODUS.

CHAPTER 1ST AND LAST.

1. Extinguisher unto St. George the Chief Ruler, and his mindless satellites :

2. Pax and reformation vobiscum !

3. Yet see I small signs of it yet, though I have taught ye freely for years past.

4.　And now that I leave, my heart yearneth toward ye, that I might take ye with me.

5.　(And drop ye on the road, that so the land of Singapura might be happy, and that the philosopher might have peace likewise.)

6.　Thou stubborn and perverse generation of Cobras—swell not out thy checks with pride, lest men, knowing ' y th se signs thy poison, should trample upon ye to ~~avoid~~ your stings.

7.　Yet can I not abide with ye longer to advise ye.

8.　Hearken, then, unto the lessons have taught ye, and ye may still be happy, and content those whom ye legislate for.

9.　And thou, St. George : Take thine hands from off the horns of that bull.

10.　Thou canst not cope with the tiger !

11.　And hast thou not but now showed unto the Juke that the bull can prevail even over the tiger ?

12.　How, then, canst thou expect to be victorious in this struggle ?

13.　Moreover, pay unto thy servants the wages due unto their labour, but appoint no man unto an office without labour merely that thou mayest thrust unearned money from the Queen's people into the pocket of a favourite !

www.ingramcontent.com/pod-product-compliance
Lightning Source LLC
Chambersburg PA
CBHW020235090426
42735CB00010B/1709